HOW TO BE A HANDMADE BOSS

EASILY SELL YOUR CRAFTS ONLINE AND BUILD A SUCCESSFUL CREATIVE BUSINESS

STEPH COLE-LEWIS

purple star design

First published in Great Britain 2022 by Purple Star Publishing

Copyright © Steph Cole-Lewis

All rights reserved. No part of this publication may be reproduced, stored in or introduced into a retrieval system, or transmitted, in any form, or by any means (electronic, mechanical, photocopying, recording or otherwise) without the prior written permission of the publisher.

The right of Steph Cole-Lewis to be identified as the author of this work has been asserted by him in accordance with the Copyright, Designs and Patents Act 1988.

This book is sold subject to the condition that it shall not, by way of trade or otherwise, be lent, resold, hired out, or otherwise circulated without the publisher's prior consent in any form of binding or cover other than that in which it is published and without a similar condition including this condition being imposed on the subsequent purchaser.

Design by Clare McCabe, www.purplestardesign.co.uk

ISBN13: 9798435334623

DISCLAIMER

The contents of this book do not constitute advice and is not intended as a substitute for professional business advice.
This book is published in good faith but neither the publisher or the author shall be held liable for any alleged damage arising from any suggestion or information contained in this book.

A Dedication

To all the bosses with an internal struggle to do something creatively against society's ideals, you're not alone. Follow the tiny voice telling you there's something more waiting for you on the other side of your comfort zone.

To my husband, Ashley. Thank you for your unwavering support and help over the last decade, for keeping me standing upright when I wanted to crumble, and for always pushing me forward.

To my mum, Teresa. Thank you for always showing me that just because someone says you can't do something, that doesn't mean you have to listen to them, and teaching me how to be a leader and a trailblazer.

To my dad, Mike. Thank you for showing me what an entrepreneurial spirit truly looks like, and that showing me that you can do anything you put your mind to, where there's a will, there's a way.

To uncle Kevin, thank you for being my silent cheerleader all these years. I'm saddened that I didn't find out how proud of me you were until after you passed away, but it means so much that you did it anyway. Rest in peace you good egg.

And finally to all of my family and friends who have supported me even in small ways over the years, you know who you are.

Index

1. Introduction 7
2. About You, Boss 25
3. Maker Mindset 35
4. Bountiful Boundaries & Great Goals 63
5. The Ideal Business Name in 24 Hours ... 93
6. Lovely Legalities 103
7. Wondering Where to Sell? 115
8. The Tantalising Trio: Target Market, Branding & Products 125
9. Perfect Packaging 169
10. Painless Pricing 177
11. Superb Storytelling 187
12. Kick-Butt Keywords & Search 197
13. Magical Yet Manageable Marketing ... 215
14. Simply Scaling + Take Your Business Further 235

WHAT ARE YOUR *thoughts?*

Chapter 1

INTRODUCTION

"If one more person calls my business "a little jewellery business" again I'm going to scream" I thought silently. I was sitting around a table of family members and friends at a birthday get-together. I'd just started my business, and it was still very early days. This was my "business debut" and quite frankly, I was not feeling my best.

I thought I would feel differently, like I was the star of the show, stepping down a long staircase in a glittery dress to a jaunty tune. Instead, I felt like I was falling down the stairs wearing a bin bag, while trumpets played in time to my bum bouncing off each step.

It had only been a couple of months earlier that I had proudly announced that I was starting a handmade jewellery business, and that I was going to sell "statement pieces". To this day, I still don't really know what the heck I was on about, so I can't blame my loved ones really.

You see, I was a bit of a serial entrepreneur, a term you might be hearing a great deal about in this book. I'd actually lost count of the number of things I had sold both online, and in person. My first "business" was when I was aged 5, when I bought a multi-pack of 100 clear rulers from Staples for £1, and took them to school to sell them for 50p each.

My dad had first put the idea in my head and had

encouraged me to go for it. He laughs about it now, but without that wacky suggestion, I probably would never have done it! I thought it was an absolutely genius idea, but as it turned out, most of the boys didn't really care about stationery, other than to flick things at each other in class, and the girls wanted pretty rulers with pink glitter and rainbow stickers on them. My ruler business went bust. Sad times.

I then went on to sell Pokemon cards when I was six years old. I had got lucky with the pack that week that I had purchased with my £1 pocket money, and had got some pretty special cards. I sold them for £5 each and made £19 profit.

(Side-note - have you seen how much the original Pokemon cards sell for these days!? I feel like I got the bum-end of the deal there!)

I continued to sell Pokemon cards until I spent my profits on more cards that ended up being boring "energy" cards that nobody wanted. That was the first time I felt business disappointment. "It's not fair!" I thought to myself. "I wanted to create a business and make money, not spend it and lose money!" Little Steph had her first taste of a business failure, and it came just at the right time.

Between the ages of 6-12 I started to learn "the art of the hustle" from my mum and dad . By day, Dad worked at an insulation firm, and then a steel company. By night (or rather, weekends) he ran a side-hustle business where he fixed up old lawnmowers, washing machines, and other household white goods, and sold them at our local market. I'd often observe as he could run his eye over a rusty piece of junk and see more potential in it. I'd just see the bin. My mum bought clothing from outlet stores, dressed them beautifully on a mannequin, and sold them for more than the original designers did in the shops or online. What a hustler!

My mum and dad also bought items from the £1 Shop and sold them at agricultural shows and fairs. It truly fascinated me how you could turn raw "ingredients" or "stock", package them differently, sell them in a different location and make more money. I didn't know how they did it, but I know one day we left the £1 Shop with two trolleys full of #swag, and they sold most of it that weekend.

One weekend made £1000 profit, that was more than my young brain could comprehend at the time. I remember sitting outside or in a poorly lit and leaky old barn, week after week, when my parents and I went to the markets or shows to sell our wares. I still remember the early mornings and frosty starts, partnered with the smell of banged-up burger vans and the taste of tea from a flask. It was here where I really learned how to be resilient, and how to actually sell something to someone.

I then took a spiritual hiatus from my own businesses (aka exams and playing my Gameboy far too much) until I was fourteen when I started to sell beads on Ebay. I know what you're thinking, and yes, fourteen is, strictly speaking, far too young to have an Ebay account... ahem... but they didn't need to know that...

I bought beads in bulk and painstakingly sold them individually online. I'd bulk order thousands of beads from places overseas like China, Singapore, Ireland and around the UK. I distinctly remember the confused look on my mum's face when the postman handed me a box so heavy that even he couldn't carry it. I tore it open on the hallway floor and carried the tiny bags individually upstairs. I took "professional" images on my iPhone 3GS (remember those?) of the individual beads and uploaded them to Ebay.

Just a piece of friendly advice, blurry photos of beads don't sell beads. Also, make sure to remove your stuffed toys from the photo background *face palm*.

I got consistent sales however, and spent my days after school wrapping endless tiny Jiffy bags of beads. I even started to get repeat customers! This actually went on for about 13 months before I had my first non-arrival case opened against me, got spooked and closed down my Ebay shop. When I had read the case, I felt like a personal failure and I wasn't cut out for it. I felt the customer's words so rawly that it honestly felt like they were standing in front of me, telling me off and spitting in my face. I sulkily navigated my way to the "close shop" button and cried as I stared at the thousands of leftover bead stocks I had accumulated.

It was short-lived though, as when I was 16, I began again, this time with clothing. I saved £50 for start-up money from my part-time job at the local hardware shop, and got the bus with a pull-about wheely trolley (yes, I did have some friends thank you for asking) to every charity shop, car boot sale and garage sale in a three-mile radius. I brought my "hauls" back and photographed them with my dad's camera, a tripod, a mannequin with a broken stand and a window as my light source. I painstakingly experimented with different angles, camera modes and lights for a solid three days.

My mum must have dreaded doing the washing when I brought back those trolleys and plastic bags full of clothes,

CHAPTER 1 : INTRODUCTION

but she silently rolled her eyes and washed them for me. I'll forever be grateful for that because quite frankly, I had no idea how to operate the washing machine *another facepalm*. This went on for two years, and I had built up a reputation on my Ebay shop, and people actually started asking me to look out for things on my travels.

When I started college in the September of 2008, although my Forensic Science course (no, really - this is what I THOUGHT I wanted to do!) was technically full-time, I had five or six free lessons each week meant for studying. You guessed it, Steph did not study. Instead, I used my bus-pass to scan every secondhand store in the area and buy more stock.

It was a blissful business, I'm sure echoing the spirit of my parents" side-hustles as I looked at something old and tired, and imagined something new, something valuable.

The downfall of this? I exhausted every source in town and supply started to dry out. Eventually I couldn't get hold of the stock any more and the business quietly phased out.

At 17 I had met my future husband during college, and at age 18, we had started another side-hustle using his talents: fixing up retro games consoles. My husband was and still is an epic nerd, and is the only person I know that will take a console completely to pieces, and love putting it back together. Go figure.

Once again, we hit the garage sales and car boot sales to find our used consoles and games and started a shop on what used to be called play.com. We were called "the posh gamers" (we really weren't) and I had attempted to build a brand with this new business. It was the first time that I had started to implement some common branding elements that you see in businesses today such as business cards, professional packaging, and the idea for our own website.

We looked on Facebook Marketplace for broken consoles and old games nobody wanted, and "flipped" them on the Marketplace for five times what we paid for them. I used to hate wrapping the oddly-shaped consoles (mainly because I cannot for the life of me wrap gifts at the best of times) and my stubborn 18-year-old self used to avoid doing it. My husband would always end up doing them and although he gave me the evil eye while doing it, I'll always appreciate what he did to help us run that side business.

Looking back, I had some really great ideas for that business, but we were just too "scared" to do them. I had wanted to open a shop where we bought and sold old games, movies, consoles, and retro spares, but as a "kid" of 18, I felt like the world looked down on me. In fact, I signed off every work email as "Stephen" because of the terrible reaction I got when I signed off with my own name. Make of that what you will.

I truly believe that if I had worked on my mindset and had got brave at this point, I would have come further ahead, faster. We could even be running that little shop now.

Regardless, we co-ran that business until we were twenty when we literally ran out of room, and again, local supplies ran dry. It didn't help either that play.com closed down! We were also starting to get "real" jobs and didn't have the time to invest into it. It was time to "grow up", but the "side-hustle spirit" never leaves you…

At 21, I ran an overstock perfume side-hustle with my mum

(sorry Mum!). We were out shopping together one day when the local hardware store was getting rid of old stock in out of date packaging for 50p each. We were the first ones there and we got into a frenzy, fast. We bought lamps, clocks, extension cords - you name it, if it had a red sticker on it, we bought it. So much so, that we had to get my dad to come and pick up our haul in his van (thanks Dad!). We went to our local market every week and sold our "stock". As our supplies began to dwindle, I started to phone around shops to solicit more. However, as we found out, if you ask shops when they are marking things down to 50p, they will probably hang up, thinking you're a prank caller, or not know the answer themselves.

It was then that the business evolved into selling perfume and other things totally unrelated to perfume. We went to our local £1 shop and bought perfumes there, then sold them for £3 at a local car boot sale. This excited me because I was finally able to get a ready supply of stock. This was the first time that I realised the power of the "target market". At some markets the perfumes sold well, while at others they didn't. When I spent hours analysing why, I observed the people walking round these markets: mostly men aged 35-55, not the ideal ladies' perfume clientèle.

I started to change where I placed things, and even took different stock to different markets. This seemed to fix the problem and the perfumes sold well until I oversaturated the nearby car boot sale and market customers, and sales ran dry.

A couple of years after, I reluctantly gave up all business ideas and side-hustles as I had started my gemology training whilst working in the jewellery trade, and had begun to live, eat and breathe everything diamond, gemstone and jewellery. It consumed me for three solid years. But I grew to hate it. What once fascinated my science-loving brain had slipped into a love-hate study-drop-out relationship.

Once again, came that itch to start up my side-hustle hobby again.

So as you can see, people had always known me as a bit of a business-head, and those businesses detailed above were just the ones I had implemented and stuck to, every month there were dozens of ideas and new ventures to go for.

But this handmade jewellery business was the first time I had felt that inner spark, it was a feeling like everything had clicked into place and I had seen a glimpse of something I desperately wanted to do. Instead of adding value with product placement and different locations, I could sell these products online, adding value with my hands, making something new out of raw parts. I couldn't help myself: I went to my jewellery box, picked up the first piece of dress jewellery I could find, and started taking it to pieces, making notes and learning as I went.

As you can now imagine, as I told various friends and family members about my handmade jewellery idea. They nodded with pursed lips and confused looks, and a few of them even carried on their days as if I'd said nothing significant at all. But this was significant to me. It had to be!

At this time, I was working four days a week in a job that sucked the soul out of me. I spent my days dusting shelves and staring at the beige walls. I sneezed through the floating dust and blistered my hands with the spray bottle of cleaning fluid. After three days at that job, I remember saying quietly to myself, "I hate it here".

But like we all do, I talked myself into staying because of the "steady paycheck" and "opportunity for climbing the ladder". As I later discovered, there was no ladder. In fact, the ladder had been pulled out from under me.

I had taken this job after being made redundant, and having found nothing else, was grateful when I received a call to say that I had got a job as assistant manager. This, as I later found out, was a lie, and I was actually doing the job of a sales assistant, and being paid accordingly. Having found this out after three months, this should probably have been my first red flag... but I digress.

The 18 months in that job were some of the darkest I had ever encountered, it still makes me shudder now. I endured hurtful comments that slashed my confidence and reduced me to tears in the stock room; promises of climbing the ladder that were never kept, and a mountain of other issues that could be a book in itself. I remember the sinking feeling of opening my first payslip and thinking, "All that sadness, upset, anger and effort... for this?" The feeling of going into work the next day was like submerging my body in an ice lake. I went numb all over, and it was as if every limb had just given up.

If you're reading this now and you can relate to what I'm saying about your own job, run like the wind.

Needless to say, by the end of those 18 months, I was a shell of a human being. I was a young woman that would once have answered the shop floor telephone with gusto and cheerfulness, now I stuttered through the simplest of "good mornings". Where I once happily wore pink lip balm and floaty dresses, I now struggled to find the energy to shower and wore slippers to work. I had been the kind of person who never got ill, and then within months, I was getting sores on my face and chest infections every other month. I wasn't happy, my body wasn't happy, my soul wasn't happy.

I'm the kind of person that believes that if you are suffering and you ignore it, your body will MAKE you listen. That's what happened in April of 2015, my body made me listen. I had been ill yet again in the days before, foods that once made me scoff them down with joy, I now struggled to keep down. I carried on working, as days off "put strain on the team" until one morning, I ran to the toilet for the fifth time that day. I stared at the porcelain bowl for what felt like hours. I sat on the floor and thought, "I wonder if I would recognise myself from two years ago?" My stomach flipped and churned inside my body, and tears began streaming down my cheeks. I felt an overwhelming urge to stand up and get the heck out. As I returned to the shop floor, I said to everyone, "I have to go home." I grabbed my stuff and ran out the door.

It's funny how we can delude ourselves into something so much that we believe it, and that day I had convinced myself it was just a tummy infection, or I'd eaten something that was having a heated disagreement with me inside my stomach.

As I hopped on the bus home, wondering if I should sit near the door so I could exit quickly if I felt poorly, I started to drift in and out of consciousness. I have no memory of what happened on that fifty-minute bus journey, but I am super grateful that I managed to wake up before my stop. When my home stop came, I had a searing pain in my lower tummy that felt like a chick was trying to hatch out from under my skin. I went straight to my local doctor's practice and got an emergency appointment. What happened afterwards is a bit of a blur. My doctor rushed me into hospital where it was discovered that my appendix was about to burst with a severe infection. The nurse at the hospital asked, "How are you not bent over in pain? People liken this kind of infection to childbirth pains!" My body had clearly been fighting it for a while, but I had been ignoring it. I had effectively disconnected with my body so much that I had disregarded the pain. I had been "brainwashed" into going about my daily life and was so out of touch with my own physical wellbeing that I didn't know what comfortable felt like any more.

I was about to be rushed into the operating theatre when a nurse said my pulse was too high, and they had to wait for my heart rate to come down. I probably should have mentioned before that I have a chronic health anxiety problem and a pretty bad fear of hospitals that did not help this process at all. Yay for the over-production of adrenaline!

I finally was stable enough after four hours to have the operation, and once I waved my family goodbye and began being wheeled down to the operating theatre, I breathed a sigh of relief and let the held-in tears finally flow down my cheek as I counted the strip lights on the ceiling. The kind nurse told me to count backwards from ten as I was put to sleep... pretty sure I only reached eight.

Once I came round, I had this overwhelming feeling that I was extremely lucky. I know that to some, an appendix-removal op would be as minor as having a tooth filling, but to me it was huge. If I had waited a few more hours, or ignored my body any longer, I could have been dealing with something much, much worse.

As I lay in the bed dazed and confused, I knew that if my days had ended there and then, I wouldn't have been happy with where I was . I would have ignored my gut feeling and better judgement for the sake of a rubbish salary.

How much does giving up your freedom, your sanity, your dreams and your health cost? £925 a month apparently. This realisation hurt more than the cuts I'd had into my stomach just hours earlier.

I was completely ashamed of myself, and at that point I declared out loud: "Something has to change".

It was in the two-week post-op recovery that I opened up my first Etsy shop. I had owned a website for my jewellery business since earlier that year, but it wasn't getting much traction at all. Quite frankly, I hadn't been in the headspace and had begun to let my dream slip away. I had put it aside to favour my 9-5, but I had already decided at that point that enough was enough, I was getting out of there.

When I was setting up my Etsy shop, I felt amazing. It was like a weight was gradually lifting off me and I had discovered my purpose and my calling once again. I went to work two weeks later with a spring in my step. I was clear on what I wanted and had a plan. I began to make slow and steady sales on Etsy and started to put more and more effort into it. However, much like my five-year-old ruler-selling self, I got frustrated when sales weren't coming in fast enough. I was beginning to feel despondent about my business, and hastily Googling "how to sell crafts online" was definitely not helping. The many damaging pieces of advice I read and implemented was for sure the cause of my shop taking one step forward and two steps back each month.

But what I did have was a compelling motivation. My hospital visit and the guilt I felt about treating myself so poorly echoed in my mind; I pushed on, and decided that I was going full-beast mode on this business. I WAS going to figure it out, and if no-one could show me, I would pave the way myself and become my own coach. That is exactly what I did. The rest, as they say, is history. And bloody good history if I do say so myself.

I'd spend every moment I could learning everything there was to know about online business, and pooling the knowledge I had already gathered from my many previous side-hustles. I compiled this all into a scraggy notebook with my goal scrawled on the first page: "to run my business full-time". This would form the basis of the formula that we will be discussing in this book, and would be the foundations for my training and coaching programmes. I worked evenings, weekends and on the commute to and from work, continuously testing, pivoting, note-taking and learning. I tried new ways to brand, price, take images, source supplies, styles, designs, target market and many more. Before long, I had the results of these tests blended with my years of experience with my side-hustles and retail training. What I had now was a strategy, a formula that I could implement into any business I had and get results. And that's what I did Christmas of 2015.

I'll never forget my first Christmas on Etsy. I woke up one morning to 30 new orders overnight (yes, money as you SLEEP!) and by the end of the year, I had made $6000+ (£4500+) in November and December alone. Nothing can prepare you for the day you realise you CAN do this. It's unlike anything I've ever experienced. People often describe it as "life just clicks and you get back control over your financial life". I was absolutely euphoric, like I'd come in from a freezing cold winter and been met with a 40-degree jacuzzi, a hot chocolate and tickets to Disneyland. It was the moment that I realised that this stuff WORKED. My "little craft business" has graduated from college and is going out into the big wide world. I was ready to jump ship and go into it full-time!

That Christmas made me realise that I was 100% going to quit my job. It was happening for real. It took me three months just to work up the courage to go into my boss's office and quit, in fact It took one of my coworkers to tell me to march upstairs and escape. Before I could change my mind, I ran up the stairs and blurted out, "If it's ok, I'd like to hand in my notice please, thanks.". We both sat there quietly and after what felt like hours of bewildered staring, my boss said, "Ok, no problem," and carried on cashing up for the day. I slowly walked downstairs, opened the door to the shop floor and didn't notice that I was beaming from ear to ear. It didn't matter that I felt like my boss didn't really care about me leaving, or that I hadn't even explained why. All I knew was that I went home that day and screamed:

"I QUIT!!"

I will always remember my first day of being a full-time business owner, I still celebrate the anniversary to this day 16th April 2016. That was the day when I breathed again, when I stopped being a shell of myself and instead embraced my dream. I'd be lying if I said it was easy all of the time. I still experimented, had days where I only had three or four orders, mixed up orders, sent broken things out in error, and couldn't cope with demand - but I was in control of all of it. After two months of doing this business full-time, I had landed a new wholesale account, made 468 Etsy orders, 97 website orders and had hired my first Virtual Assistant to help with social media and other general tasks I didn't have time to do any more.

This trajectory has only continued since. Because of my Handmade business, I have been able to buy our first home, purchase my dream car, and move twice. I've plastered rooms, replaced bathrooms and kitchens, and built dream home offices. I go on fabulous vacations, work when I want to, (hello midweek cinema trips!) and endless amounts of other freedoms that I've hustled hard to give myself. To be honest, I can't even say I've worked "hard" in the traditional sense, and that in itself will be a mindset issue we talk about later in this book. Instead, I have worked smarter, with more patience and simplicity. Don't get me wrong, there will be days when you just want to throw in the towel and give up, days where you feel like whatever you do just won't work, and times when you question if this was all just a stupid idea. Successful business owners are those that have the tenacity, determination and courage to push through, rest when they need to rest, and ride the wave of creativity when they can.

Because of my business I was able to start my YouTube channel in 2019 and to start sharing videos, and coaching handmade business owners through the same struggles I encountered. With "The Handmade Bosses Success Academy", I've helped hundreds of handmade business owners (that I affectionately call "Bosses") to break through their own barriers and make the returns they want from their business. Whether it's money, freedom, time, energy or simply to pursue something creative, I love helping handmade business owners become their own boss through my coaching business, Handmade Bosses. My passion is to help people find that special gift (that we all have) and bring it to the world.

The reason why my previous businesses failed and why my handmade business succeeded has a remarkable resemblance to building a house. You see, businesses that are built in a rush, that cut corners and throw out proven principles in favour of new ones, to put it nicely, are built on shaky foundations and sooner or later (usually within the first 18 months) will fall and leave a heap of dusty bricks and a hot mess in their wake. But if you take the time to learn the foundations, build a solid base that you work up from, then your business will continue to stand for years. That's what you will find in this book, the foundational knowledge you need to start building your business. Even seasoned sellers often forget the foundational knowledge, and sometimes have been on the brink of collapse before we have begun working together.

I wanted to write this book to dispel some of the terrible advice I have seen floating around on the grandiose world wide web, and to help you start to build the strong foundations that your business will need to grow on. I wanted to share with you for the small price of this book, some principles that other handmade business coaches charge thousands of dollars for, mainly because I know sometimes the price of entry into the "business club" can be extreme, and I want to help you to get started and begin bringing in income from your business.

The main goal for you reading this book is not only to increase your income, but to start to gain confidence in how and why you run your business the way you do, because hey, we weren't born knowing how to run a business! I'd love to help you lay those important foundations (and strengthen your existing ones!) so that your business can stand the test of time and continue to grow and expand year after year.

CHAPTER 1 : INTRODUCTION

Throughout this journey we are about to embark on together, you'll understandably want to take notes and refer back to various chapters again and again. That's why when creating this book, we decided to make a book/workbook hybrid. There are spaces for all-important breakthroughs and ideas, and I encourage you to write in the spaces, dog-ear the pages, highlight important points and doodle on the front page, if that gets your creative juices flowing - I promise I won't be offended. In fact, show me your #messyaf copy and tag me @handmadebosses - I'd love to see it!

So Boss, are you set? Get your thumbs at the ready and turn that page.

Get your book bonuses here:

WHAT ARE YOUR *thoughts?*

Chapter 2

ABOUT YOU, BOSS

This book is dedicated to you, Boss. But let's take a step back and appreciate you (because I bet you don't do that too often!)

You picked up this book because you know deep down that you're destined for more. Maybe you have dreamily looked at a strong-looking women at a craft fair, donning an apron and battling to take money fast enough to meet demand at her stall, while you've thought, "I would LOVE to be in her shoes right now."

Perhaps it was the painful goodbyes you say to your child while you wave at them through the early morning grogginess and yet again set off for another mundane day at the office.

Or could it be that this book appealed to you because of the boss that drives you insane, with constant micro-managing, underappreciation and hurtful, backhanded compliments?

Whatever it was that inspired you to explore starting or growing your own handmade business, you've taken a step that 95% of others don't. You'd better believe that you are already four steps ahead of any possible competition, just by taking the time to read this single page. Even by browsing your local bookstore, or searching for this book online, you have pushed aside all of the naysayers and not-so-helpful comments from Aunty June, and decided to go all-in and bet on yourself. Let me tell you, that bet has ridiculously high odds.

You're probably at the very beginning of your journey, less than a year in business, and you are consuming all the information you can so that you can giga-brain your business and learn from others' mistakes from the get-go. You have an inkling of what you can make, and what you'd like to make that has sparked an exciting chain reaction in you. So much so that you probably find it hard to switch off "business thinking" at the end of the day. Or you may be a little way into your journey, but know you can do better, and you want to learn more. Wherever you are in your journey Boss, it's great to have you here - pull up a chair, get comfortable, let's talk about you!

It's not easy taking the first step on your way to your dream, idea, or business opportunity. Sometimes everything can seem against us, even before we have even started. Circumstances may have given us a mindset and inner voice that's constantly trying to keep us in our comfort zone, but I implore you to keep going, and follow your gut feeling which led you to this book.

I like to imagine that negative voice as a little comfort zone gremlin with a bad attitude, a rope around his waist waiting to lasso you back in the comfort zone; he stinks to high heaven and is named Negative-Nelly. Feel free to name and imagine your gremlin as you wish, but putting a face to a feeling, and a name to that face makes that voice just a bit less scary. Nelly is a ginormous pain in the butt to put it politely, and is always just "there", ready to pounce the moment you doubt yourself.

Nelly can often say things like:

"No-one will want to buy what you make!"

"Who do you think you are, starting a business and playing shop?"

"You can't charge what you need to, so what's the point?"

"People are already doing it so much better than you, you'll never reach the level they have."

"It all looks so complicated, you can never learn it all."

"I hate your face."

These ugly thoughts can swirl around our head constantly, and if you haven't experienced them yet, believe me, you will. There's a Negative-Nelly in all of us.

Despite Nelly's voice swirling in your mind, there's also the Positive-Penny voice. I imagine this voice as the best version of yourself. You know that day when your hair was on point, your eyebrows kicked ass, your mind was clear, you were quick-witted, you felt fierce and overall just felt like a 10/10 badass? That's your Positive-Penny voice. She sits within you, ready to remind you to keep going. She's the one that chimes in every now and again with your big Why - your reason for starting this craft business in the first place.

Penny will say things like:

"Come on, keep going, you can do this!"

"You had a 5* feedback this week - good job!"

"You should be proud of yourself for taking all those photos!"

"Despite not having ticked everything off your list, you did three things out of five - amazing job!"

After having worked with hundreds of handmade business owners at the time of writing, I can tell you that every single one of them has a strong reason why they want to pursue a handmade business. It's the single biggest driving force behind their decision to take the big leap. The best people I work with have a fire under their butt so hot that I can almost feel the heat through the video call or live workshop. Stay tuned as this is something that we will be discussing in the next chapter. This driving force is the only thing that will differentiate the people who listen to Nelly or Penny - either giving up, or keeping going.

When working with craft businesses or handmade business owners wanting to take their business online, I often observe one of the six traits detailed below. I'm willing to bet that at least one of the following is true for you; if so, which?

1. You're a serial creative. Yes, you flit from one project to another, but you're always looking at things a bit differently to others. Others see a tube of potato chips, you see a new pen holder. They see an empty pasta sauce jar, you see a doorstop. They see an old car battery, you see a... well, a car battery. Some things are just what they are.

2. You know there's MORE than this. Whether you're in a 9-5 beavering away under fluorescent tube lighting, or you spend your days taking care of little monsters and treading on rogue bits of Lego, it's a daily occurrence

CHAPTER 2 : ABOUT YOU, BOSS

that you look out the window and hear that nagging whisper that says, "You know you can do more, right?"

3. You like money. There, now we can all relax, the elephant in the room has had a bit of spotlight! To like money is not bad, careless or crummy, it's a completely natural desire. Often, as creatives, we feel as if we shouldn't be allowed to WANT to make more money from something that comes so easily to us. And even if we do, we always have a mental follow-up that sounds something like this: "If I make an extra £10,000 this year, I'll spend most of it on the kids anyway, so I'm not a bad person!"

4. There's a part of you that's a bit of an introvert. You like the idea of selling your goods online through a site such as Etsy and Amazon Handmade. You love the idea of getting money straight into your bank with as little human interaction as possible.

5. You want an upgraded lifestyle. You know there are parts of your life that you wish you could upgrade, but you feel like you "should" earn it. You yearn to be able to take an all-inclusive bouji holiday to Hawaii. You would love to replace the old car that doesn't unlock when it's below six degrees. It would feel amazing to be able to spend less time in the 9-5 grind and more time with your loved ones. It's not like you want to buy a private island, a gold-plated iPhone and a 6-berth yacht, you just want the ability to think, "I want that... let's do it!"

6. You're a bit of a serial entrepreneur. You have had more than three businesses (or business ideas), and now fancy doing something a bit different. You have had this

"feeling" to do something creative for a while, and your current business/job has just lost its creative appeal. Or you could just fancy doing something different, after all, we're not living in the 1920s where you stayed in a job for life. We have the ability to switch and change up as often as we desire. Your favourite phrase is, "I could do that!"

All in all, you are someone that is willing to get stuck in and start your journey. You may have experienced some push-back from friends and family members, and that's okay; you know that in spite of what they say, you just need to carry on. What if Walt Disney, Richard Branson or Elon Musk had given up the minute someone said to them, "Hey, this here is a dumb idea"? Then we wouldn't be watching those movies that capture our hearts and imagination; we wouldn't have the benefit of an airline that takes us to far-flung places with style and luxury and we wouldn't be able to drive clean electric cars that go further. Everyone you admire started from zero and had haters along the way.

You have probably had some truly awful advice in the past from self-proclaimed "business gurus" that have given you outdated and damaging guidance. In one instance, a student of mine had spent $997 on a course that had actually damaged her Etsy shop to such an extent that it took six months before her business sales and reputation came back to life again. It's a scary thought, and one no business owner relishes. It's a sad reality that anyone can throw up a blog, website or videos and call themselves an expert. Even worse, taking advice from those who are not where you want to be is the worst thing any new business owner can do.

But this isn't the only mistake I see handmade business owners making. Below are some of the top six mistakes (believe me, there were more!) that I see most commonly:

1. Making the product first, then reverse-engineering the business around it. Let's be honest, most of us are here because we started to make something, and then we (or a loved one) said, "Hey, we should sell this online!" Then we proceeded to throw up a website or an Etsy shop, list ten items and just waited for the sales to come in, Wolf of Wall Street style.

2. Focusing on marketing too much. Yes, I know - it would make sense for a business owner to care about marketing, and when I asked some of our previous students what they thought, they said that in the beginning, they had been searching solely for marketing advice. However, a big mistake that handmade business owners make is that they drive all this traffic to a shop that isn't geared toward that type of traffic. So it's like herding sheep into a paddock with a fence missing (more on this later!)

3. Being impatient and panic-changing. If I had a £1 for every time this happened, I could probably afford to have a Scrooge McDuck-sized cavern of gold coins. When online craft businesses first start out, they have an image in their mind of money flowing effortlessly and easily into their bank account, yet they panic when they don't get sales for three weeks. Instead of having confidence in their abilities (more on this in the book) and changing things that would benefit them, they Google "How to make more sales on Etsy" and action the first piece of guidance given, effectively rendering

all their previous hard work wasted.

4. Working on the wrong thing. Many business owners feel their way around their problems in business. They will think or say, "I feel like Instagram isn't working for me"; "I think my email list isn't growing fast enough"; "I feel like I should change my branding". This is a dangerous game. Our feelings change seventeen times a day at best: altering your business based on feelings is treacherous territory.

5. Having a bad mindset. This wins top spot in my opinion. Everything we do comes from our brain. If we're sad, we have a sad face. If we're happy, we walk happily. If we find something hilariously funny, we can't help but stifle a laugh (remember you always found something REALLY funny when you had to be quiet for school exams?) All of this comes from our mood and mindset, and running our business is no different. If you are in an anxious or worried mood, you're a hundred times more likely to make business decisions out of panic than if you are content and happy. If you're still not convinced, remember that all businesses that failed did so because of an ultimate decision someone made - these bad decisions can be altered if we change our mindset (more on this soon!)

6. Over-complicating is a form of procrastination. This one is super-duper important. If you get nothing else from this chapter, make sure you take this away. Over-complicating things is truly a form of procrastination. Listen up Boss, having a handmade business doesn't have to be hard, in fact, when it's easier, it makes everything flow so much more simply. Whenever you

find yourself wanting to add unnecessary bells and whistles to something that should otherwise be easy, stop. Ask yourself, have I been taught that to reach my goals I need to work harder? Is this why I'm making this more difficult than it has to be?

Throughout this book, I will be sharing with you the easy and uncomplicated way of doing things. You won't see me sharing over-the-top SEO strategies or marketing madness, but instead I will be sharing how to start your business with a huge sense of calm and ease.

Ultimately, the above mistakes will stunt your growth and effectively add years onto your journey to your ultimate goal. Many future handmade bosses think they can figure it out along the way and go it alone. "I can Google this stuff" or "I'll work it out when I get there" are just some of what I hear or read. When I see people in this frame of mind, I often follow them on social media and check back in a few months later - sadly, 80% of these businesses have disappeared within that time frame. It's far better for you to know what I'm going to teach you in this book beforehand, than to arrive at a time when you need it, forget about this book, and take panic-action.

Now for some more "you-love". Boss, you have everything you need to accomplish your goal already hanging out inside you. In this book we are going to take a journey together to get you toward your goal of having a successful online handmade business - and let me tell you, if you put your all into it, it will be the best journey ever.

I just want to thank you so much for choosing to take this journey with me. I love working with handmade business owners whether one-to-one, through my live masterclasses or through words on a page. It's truly my honour that you're reading this right now!

And don't forget to download the book bonuses at www.handmadebosses.com/bookbonus full of handy maker tools, resources and video trainings for you to have alongside this book!

WHAT ARE YOUR *thoughts?*

Chapter 3

MAKER MINDSET

Mindset is one of those buzzwords that has been thrown around over the last decade, it can be used loosely in other ways such as:

- psyche
- ethos
- frame of mind
- mood
- mentality
- way of thinking
- thought process

The words we use to describe it all mean the same, but it circles around one fact: as humans we have emotions and feelings and these are a result of our mood and mindset at any one moment, and it can change multiple times a day. Being able to control and alter our mindset to a certain extent is a skill that all successful business owners have, because the quality of our work, decisions and therefore our business depends on it.

Understanding mindset and how it affects your business is ultimately the biggest skill you need to learn as a handmade boss. As mentioned previously, whether we do something well or not is 70% mindset and 30% skill. Yes, if you play a round of football you have to practise and learn certain skills, but if you enter the field not believing you can do it, then you may as well go home and give up.

This usually is a self-perpetuating cycle; we aren't feeling fantastic so we don't bring our A-game, we don't bring our A-game because we don't feel fantastic.

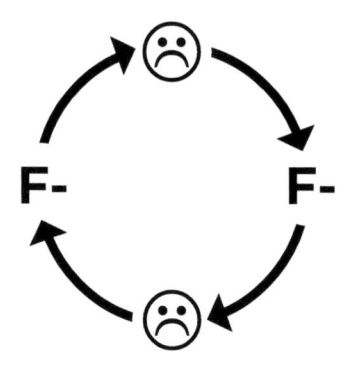

F- F-

I probably don't need to explain why this is so important in the daily running and planning of your business, but just in case you're not convinced that this is more important than marketing, SEO skills and pricing, then here's a better way to think of what having a bad mindset does to your business:

Sabotaging Business Loop

- have negative thoughts
- reactionary thoughts of feeling hopeless, down or useless
- you take an action in your business that isn't your best work
- this action fails or doesn't perform as well as hoped. This leaves you feeling worse

This is showing what I like to call a "sabotaging business loop". You can see clearly that it's a terrible cycle to get into, and one that can be worse for your business than an army tank ripping through your workspace.

On the other hand, if you can focus your attention and control your thoughts, you can not only get yourself out of this damaging cycle, but prevent yourself from ever getting into it. Another more urgent way to think about this loop is that it's actually a money-suck from your business. Put it this way: you aren't going to be making £10,000 business decisions when you feel this bad! In fact, many business owners get stuck in the loop for so long that they end up losing money, their business flops and they end up believing it's due to other factors at play. They blame algorithms, the competition, pricing issues and the next-door neighbours' dog, instead of just embracing that their mindset was the culprit.

You may be at the stage right now where you think one of the following:

- "It's too saturated, I can't win on that platform"
- "I can't charge £30 for my candles, no-one will pay that!"
- "I'm not very good at writing, so my descriptions will always suck"
- "I'm rubbish at tech, so I can't open a website to sell my items".

All these are thoughts that potentially could get you back into that sabotaging business loop, and get you on the fast track to failure in your business. Yes, this sounds dramatic, and you might be reading this thinking, "Jeez, I'm only two chapters in and it's already got serious," but as a coach who's worked with hundreds of businesses, I can tell you for certain that Yes, it is that dramatic, and Yes, that loop will cause your business to deteriorate.

The difference between those that succeed and those that don't is that the ones that succeed will recognise when they are in the sabotaging business loop, and know how to get themselves out of it as soon as possible. Therefore, it's a key skill you need to be able to harness as soon as possible. Practising this skill means that you have a better business, you are able to stop a "bad day" in its tracks and overall, just be 70% better at anything we put our minds to.

We all have days where everything feels just that little bit harder than it should be. In fact, studies have shown that if you believe you are having a bad day, it becomes a self-fulfilling prophecy. Your kids throw cereal on your shoe, you break a plate, your car starts making that weird noise again, you forgot to put mascara on, your shirt is inside out and you're late to work - all before 9am! We then go through our day saying, "I'm having a bad day" and what happens? You have an even worse day going forward, because your brain believes, and therefore picks up on, more reasons for this to become a bad day.

What about that person (yes, we all know one) who seems to be just plain lucky. They win money on scratch cards, get undercharged for their groceries, get away with no parking tickets and win at everything they try their hand at. Shockingly, a large portion of this "luck" can be put down to mindset too.

Top-dogs in the science industry believe that this is due to our Reticular Activating System or RAS for short.

Have you ever bought a new car in a specific colour, only to start seeing that car in that colour everywhere? You think, "Ah, I must have been the trendsetter for this car" or "I'm seeing my car everywhere, it must be popular now". In actual fact, it's not that there are more of that car on the road, but that your brain is recognising more of them, because it's tuned into it more now. Before, your brain was effectively filtering out the stuff that didn't matter to you.

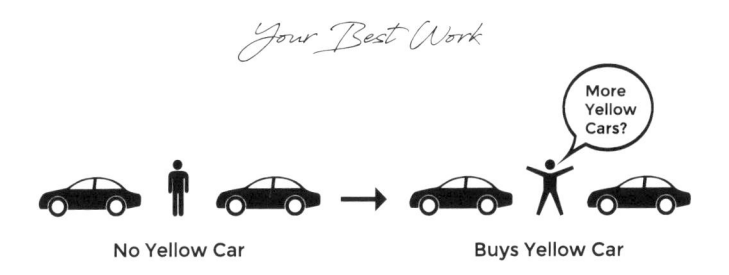

Your Best Work

No Yellow Car → Buys Yellow Car — More Yellow Cars?

This is actually a great thing because it means that once we turn our attention to our mindset and cultivating a great headspace, we are more attentive and open to opportunities and making great decisions. This comes in handy when we are so focused on a goal or a task in our business, that all we notice are things that will get us closer to that goal, and all we're thinking is how we can absolutely achieve it. When this happens, there is no stopping us; every obstacle is minor, every setback is temporary, and every small achievement is pure bliss.

There are actually some common types of mindset issues and factors that you will encounter in your handmade business journey; some will feel minor, while others will stunt your business growth for months. Understanding what they are, and what mindset wizardry is at work will help you overcome them quicker.

SABOTAGING THOUGHT PATTERNS

This is the most common and overarching theme of most mindset issues. If you just master one, make this the one you master. Sabotaging thought patterns are basically thoughts that perpetuate this cycle:

Sabotaging Business Loop

- have negative thoughts
- Sabotaging thought patterns
- reactionary thoughts of feeling hopeless, down or useless
- you take an action in your business that isn't your best work
- this action fails, or doesn't perform as well as hoped. This leaves you feeling worse

They are usually internal thoughts and dialogue that we have with ourselves and can come from external and internal programming. This is just a fancy way of explaining that we are what we think, and sometimes what other people think of us.

Take Jenny. She has a handmade business that sells jewellery. She is a bit of an introvert who loves to sit in her workspace creating clay jewellery and listen to music. She has always been described as someone who is very talented, but that isn't very good at technology. She has an Etsy shop but procrastinates doing online housekeeping to her shop. She constantly mentally repeats what her mum used to say to her: "You're very good at what you do, but technology is clearly not your friend," and uses this as an excuse if people ask her why she's not more successful with her jewellery. She is frustrated that her shop isn't growing fast enough and posts comments in groups asking for shop feedback. Whenever someone advises her to list more items and to take better images, she retorts with "Yes, but it's hard for me, I'm not very good at technology!" She then moves on to the next comment, hoping she will find something different to change in her shop to make it better. She has repeated this internal dialogue so much that it has become a mindset issue, almost to the extent of becoming a mantra.

Because of this "I can never understand technology" mindset, Jenny:

- won't learn how to use her phone camera fully, and even avoids looking at the manual
- doesn't update her shop with new branding because she is scared to "mess it up"
- doesn't want to change any titles or tags in case it messes up her traffic
- doesn't have any social media networks apart from Facebook, because she doesn't think she will be able to learn them
- never upload any updates or new products because she doesn't know how to

You can see how a flippant comment from a friend, family member, yourself or even someone online, can set off a chain reaction that can change the course of your business life. This might seem extreme, but you can replace "being afraid of technology" with any example, and you get the same result.

Even the people who you spend the most time with can have a major impact on your thoughts, and therefore your business. If you are spending time with those that lift your spirits and encourage you to do what it takes to reach your dreams, chances are you are going to overcome hurdles easier, take more risks and come to your business with a positive outlook. Yet, if you hang out with Negative Nellys who moan about how bad their life is and do nothing about it, who degrade you for following your dreams and complain about everything, then you are probably going to be in a bad frame of mind when working on your business. This is why in our own community (hosted within a Facebook group) we don't tolerate Negative Nellys. There are plenty of other groups for that on the internet.

I received so much feedback on this that I've outlined below a list of red flags that can warn you that people with these traits may be bringing your mindset down, and directly pushing you into the sabotaging business loop:

- they moan about their lives but do nothing to change their situation
- they only reach out to you to complain
- they judge you for wanting to change your life, or even mock you
- they are constantly saying that money is tight, then proceed to go and book expensive vacations
- they are two-faced
- you feel more drained than a can of lentils when you see them.

Another place to watch out for sabotaging thought patterns is when you talk about money; this is called "money mindset". It's estimated that 60% of people don't like talking about money, and don't want to look at their bank accounts. This in itself can start off an internal thought pattern that can sound like this:

- "I'm not good at handling finances" - you'll end up being terrible at handling finances.
- "I can't charge that, it's too much!" - you'll end up undercharging and not being profitable.
- "I never pay bills on time" - you'll end up with late fees from unpaid bills.
- "They owe me money, but I can't chase them for payment" - you'll end up with hundreds of pounds being owed to you that you'll never see again.

The fact is that the more we hide away our sabotaging thought patterns, whether about money or anything else, the more power we give it over us. It becomes the "he who shall not be named" of our minds.

This all sounds super scary and important, but how do we fix this? Well, basically, we need a brain detox. We need to identify sabotaging thoughts and patterns, find where they came from, stop it from ever happening again and find our real truth.

Below are some steps to overcome and gracefully exit the sabotaging business loop:

1. **Bring your BS into the limelight.** Dig deep and recognise any negative thoughts, beliefs or internal dialogue that you tell yourself daily. Write them down as soon as you think of them.

2. **Find the origin story.** Where did this belief come from? When? How? From who? From what situation?

3. **Find an alternative meaning.** When you recognise where you got the belief from, is there another way

you could look at it? Another story that you didn't see at the time? A person you have to forgive and let go of? Yes, this is deeeeeep, but so is your desire to have a better life, right?

4. **Flip the script**. Write down in all its glory, the dialogue, message, or belief again. Is there a different way to look at this? If you said the opposite, what would it say?

5. **Create another mantra.** We know that repetitive negative thoughts become negative mantras; we can't change our mindset overnight, so create a positive mantra for you to think/say instead.

So let's run Jenny through this. Jenny writes down her thoughts of "I'm not very good at technology." She then discovers that the origin story wasn't her mother's words, but in fact a school report from when she was seven years old. She remembers that computers were new in her school library, and that the teacher was trying to get her to understand how to make a digital robot move across the screen. She couldn't quite understand how to get it to move in the direction she wanted, and the teacher teased and said, "Maybe you just don't understand computers!" This went on her report card.

Jenny thinks of an alternative meaning: "At seven years old, programming/coding is an advanced skill. I don't blame myself for not understanding it. Anyway, I don't need to understand coding at seven years old. Maybe the teacher was projecting her own technophobic insecurities onto me. I'm fine with technology - just not coding!"

She forgives her teacher and respects her for doing the best she could. She then flips "I'm not good at technology" with "I'm great with technology! I can learn anything!" and repeats this daily to herself, and even writes it in her journal.

This is a process that I have used for years to turn negative beliefs into positive ones. I hope you will take the time to go through the steps and stop these negative thought patterns from doing any more damage.

Coaching Questions:

What are some sabotaging thought patterns you have?

What negative thoughts pop into your head daily or weekly?

Looking back, what are some actions you have taken in your life as a result of feeling rubbish, that you have later regretted?

What are some comments that other people have said to you that keep coming up in your mind?

What are some negative business beliefs you have that are holding you back?

Where did this thought really come from?

What is a different way of looking at this?

How can you flip the script?

What will be your new mantra?

COMFORT ZONE

When you think of the word comfort, it probably conjures up images of fleecy blankets, cups of coffee, books, your spot on the couch and '90s laundry softener adverts. THIS type of comfort is great. When you think of your comfort zone though, that is an entirely different story.

Our comfort zone is a psychological state where someone has their basic needs met, has no risk involved and has a limited set of habits and behaviours that tend to deliver the same outcome. All that is just a fancy way of saying you're not going to put yourself "out there", because why would you? You have it great where you are now. It's likened to being in your PJs on a Saturday night with a tub of ice-cream and a movie you've seen a hundred times. You know how the evening will play out, but you don't mind. After all, you did change the ice-cream flavour, that's daring enough.

But just as our comfort zone lulls us into a controlled, snuggly, warm environment with teddy bears and unicorns, it has a more sinister undertone: you won't achieve your dreams within your comfort zone. Why? Well, have you achieved your dreams yet? What you have done before will get you to where you are now, you have to do something completely different to get to where you need to go, AKA step out of your comfort zone.

Many Bosses struggle with this reality. Starting a business is full of anxiety, worries and stresses not ordinarily found in everyday life. It can be really easy to say, "Nope, I'm out!" and rush back to your comfort zone. In fact, I like to call it the comfort zone gremlin. These gremlins are looking for ways to get you back into the snuggle zone constantly. Got negative feedback? You want to hide under the duvet. Need to pay to learn from someone who has overcome your challenges before? Nope, I don't need to do that. Got a difficult order to finish asap? Nah, you go tidy up instead - it's still productive! *Rolls eyes* As you can see, the comfort zone is a sneaky business, and can be disguised as other things.

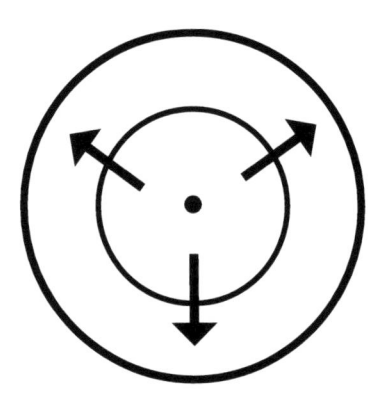

In an ideal world, you would be able to instantly recognise when it's an actual feeling of panic or anxiety and there's a very real threat involved when you leave your comfort zone, but sometimes it's not always easy to identify, which is why we often stay in the comfort zone and instead, pretend we're happy with what we have.

It takes a brave person to say, "No! I know I can do more, that I'm destined for more and that I can push myself to achieve my dreams. Bye-bye comfort zone!" And while many of us are excited and motivated at the beginning, things start to take a downturn when we find ourselves at our first hurdle.

If we stay within our cuddle zone, we never actually do anything different to get to where we need to go. In reality it may look like this:

- never uploading those new product images because you're worried they won't sell
- not reaching out to that blogger because you have never done it before
- never hiring a professional photographer because you think your cousin can work a phone camera better than a professional
- stopping halfway through writing your book because it felt too nerve-wracking (yep, I did that with this book!)
- not booking that dream holiday because... ew... bugs.

So all in all, you end up stuck with the same habits, and doing the same things, which is great if you are living your dream life right now, but not so great if you aren't.

Here are some steps to coax yourself out of your comfort zone:

1. **Reframe the boundary.** Rather than visualising getting out of your comfort zone as an actual barrier you have to cross, focus on expanding the zone to include all the activities and things you know you have to do. What if your comfort zone could include cold emailing influencers (someone who has a following of a specific niche of people, that may have a power to affect buying habits by endorsing something) to feature your products? Doing Facebook ads or launching new products?

2. **Manage risk.** When you're struggling to get out of your comfort zone (which can absolutely disguise itself as a difficult decision) try identifying worst-case scenarios. What would you do if the influencer emailed you back with a firm "no"? What would you do if you ran Facebook ads and they didn't work? What about quitting your job? Write a "Plan B" style plan.

3. **Tip-toe rather than jump.** Put a toe outside of your comfort zone rather than jumping headfirst into it. Can you comment on that influencer's image first? Send them a message to say how you appreciate their work? What about boosting a Facebook post for £1 rather than running a Facebook ads campaign? Take small steps.

4. **Connect with your body.** Your body holds real wisdom that we often take for granted. The big problem with getting outside our comfort zone is that we don't quite know how to identify a real danger (what will actually hurt us) vs a perceived threat (what we think will hurt us but won't). It takes some quiet time daily and without distraction to connect with your body. How do you feel? What sensations do you feel? Then think about a food you absolutely hate. What feelings come up for you? What points toward this food being a firm "no" for you? This is the feeling we get when we're about to make a huge mistake. Learn it, understand it and tune into it.

Coaching Questions:

What are some things that are in your comfort zone?

What are some things outside of your comfort zone?

Do things outside of your comfort zone have a real inherent risk?

What's the worst-case scenario that would happen if you went ahead with these things?

What's the best-case scenario if you went ahead with these things?

What are some small steps you can take to start to expand your comfort zone?

COMPARISON

The words "comparison is the thief of joy" is something that rings so true with handmade business owners. We research and learn by going online and seeing what our competitors are doing, but often this leads to a sense of hopelessness when you see that your competitors are doing everything right, and you can't understand or see just how they do it. Even worse, you look at your own business and think "There's no difference; how come I'm not getting the same number of sales as them!?"

We have all had that sinking feeling when our mind starts to flood with thoughts like:

- "I'll never be as good as them"
- "They're undercharging and I cannot compete"

- "They have a massive social media following, there's no way I can get that many people"
- "They seem to be doing lots of things wrong but still get sales!"
- "Why can they get away with doing that, and I can't?"

Honestly, this is one of the quickest ways to kill a good mindset, and although I encourage active research and a perception of what others in your space are doing, it's not meant as a comparison exercise. Rather, it's intended to see what is and isn't working in your space. Many business owners fall at this hurdle because they're too quick to take business personally, and let it mean something about themselves as a person, rather than just a weakness in their behaviour or knowledge, both of which can be altered if desired.

Crafters create their products from hand, they are super involved in the business and care a great deal about it (naturally). However, while this means you have ten times the strengths and skills of traditional business owners (such as dropshippers or service-based businesses) it also means that we are pre-dispositioned to take criticism of any type personally. So even if this criticism comes from our own selves, a loved one, or a seemingly successful shop that sells the exact same item as we have but has 35,783 sales, it can make us feel like a personal failure. The biggest issue here is that this way of thinking can push us into a sabotaging business loop. Instead, we have to understand that although our businesses are operated through us, we can change our behaviours and knowledge to pivot this if we wanted, all in all meaning we can change, and we should if we feel a strong sense to.

Here are some ways to stop bad comparison:

1. **Disconnect personal achievements from business achievements.** Just because you didn't meet your sales target this month and your competitor did, it does not mean anything about you as an individual. All it means is that you may need to change some strategies and learn more about how to reach this goal. Just because your competitor has 356 products in their catalogue doesn't mean you have to as well. If you are making six sales a week, and your competitor is making 78, then that means one thing, you're not quite there yet, but you will be.

2. **You don't know what goes on behind the scenes.** I receive a great deal of DMs, emails and comments asking this one question: "How come X competitor can do Y, and still get sales, and yet I'm doing it the right way and getting nothing?" Here's the reality of the situation: you only see an outward-facing view of their business - basically, what they want you to see. You don't know what goes on behind the scenes. For example, they may have hired a PR firm, been featured in a highly sought-after publication, have 50,000+ followers on social media or have spoken at an event. You don't (and won't ever) know this for sure.

3. **Don't try to hack your competitors' businesses.** Following on from my previous point, if you try to emulate your competitors' business/shop from just copying what you seeing them doing, you're only seeing a surface level view of things, and you don't know the reasoning behind it.

4. **Understand what's really going on.** Are you truly just innocently comparing your business to others? Or are you really trying to find a way to prove your business isn't as good as theirs by following along with a sabotaging thought pattern? Run yourself through the previous exercises to find out.

5. **Use it as proof of concept.** If you are viewing a store that's had substantially more orders than you, great! That means that people want that product, and if they can do it, so can you. Embrace it, print it out and save it to your dream board. This could be YOU in a few months.

Coaching Questions:

What competitors have your compared yourself to recently?

What business "failures" have you made personal?

Why are you really comparing yourself to your competitors?

Would you like a business like theirs?

Why?

BURNOUT

Burnout has begun to become mainstream with more and more creatives beginning to learn and open up about burnout and its effects. Burnout is a long-term exhaustion that can be caused by being in a state of long-term stress. It's becoming more widespread and common as we undertake more and more in our lives, and as more stress becomes acceptable and considered the "norm". When we first experience stress, it's more short term and can come in shorter intense bursts. On the other hand, burnout is when we have an extended period of stress that eventually completely wipes us out. If you need a visual idea of what burnout is like, imagine you're a lit match. Now imagine someone throwing a bucket of water over you, breaking you in half and rubbing you in dirt.

I believe a little bit of stress is actually a good thing, and I've found that as long as it's controlled, it can make us hyper-productive, resourceful and reignite our passion. However, being "bored" in your comfort zone of having extreme stress is definitely not where you want to be.

Comfort Zone	Mild anxiety	Stress	Burnout danger zone	Burnout

I probably don't need to explain why you should avoid burnout, but just in case, the reality is this: burnout can make you physically and mentally unwell, and therefore this affects your business, but more importantly, your wellbeing suffers. Hardly the best mindset for building a legacy in the form of your handmade business, Boss.

I've suffered true burnout twice in my life, and luckily, I've learned to recognise the warning signs. These may wildly differ for you, but personally, I experience the below:

- Feeling like your mindset is starting to slip. Your habits take a nosedive, you stop taking inventory of how you talk to yourself, and you stop taking days off.
- You start to make more mistakes. You begin to make silly mistakes and can't quite understand why.

- Your body starts to let you know. This varies from person to person, but I know I'm approaching burnout when I get a dull thumping headache for days, or when I start to get ill frequently.
- You feel empty. An unfulfilled feeling can make you question everything, you may not be sure why you have it, or where it's come from, but the feeling is still there.
- Having little interest in creating. Handmade business owners are natural creatives; if you are dreading creating anything, it's time to ask some serious questions.
- Thinking about work when you're not at work. We have all been guilty of this at some point, but when it becomes chronic, it's time to unplug.
- Speak to a professional. If you're not feeling quite right, speak to a healthcare professional as soon as possible.

Burnout is a scary thing, and it shouldn't be taken lightly. But luckily, if you recognise the signs early on, you can stop it in its tracks. Below are some of my favourite ways to help myself when I suffer true burnout:

1. **Unplug.** We live in a world where everyone wants a piece of our attention. If it's not kids, the dog, the cleaning or our jobs, it's social media, the news or just about any website online. All of this can actually be really damaging to our sense of self and can very quickly lead to burnout. Take time to turn your phone off, or use the "do not disturb" function.

2. **Get back to creating just for you.** Shocker: you don't have to monetise every hobby. Get back to being creative just for yourself. Make your favourite candle, create a collage, or even just create a nice home-

cooked meal. Do anything that engages your creative brain, without waking up your business brain too.

3. **Know what relaxes you.** You may not enjoy massages, shopping or lunches out, but instead enjoy beach walks, reading a book or baking a cake. Understand what relaxation looks like to you and schedule in time to perform those activities. No. Questions. Asked.

4. **Do nothing.** No really, do nothing more. Remember when you were a kid and your anthem for the summer holidays was "I'm bored!" As adults we seem to forget how to be bored. Boredom breeds ideas, relaxation and intuitive thinking. It also forges that body/mind connection.

5. **Organise yourself.** Once you start to think you can return to work again, begin by organising the heck out of your life. List your way through your day and if anything pops into your head, write it down. It may sound counterintuitive to make a list longer than Santa's, but once you get these things out of your head and onto the page, you will no longer feel like you have to hold mental space for them.

Coaching Questions:

Do you unplug often?

What truly relaxes you?

When can you schedule these things often?

How can you feel more organised in your day-to-day life?

What are your extreme stress or burnout signs to look out for?

How will you ensure that you don't burn out?

Your mindset is something you have to care for like a newborn puppy: treat it right, move it softly and give it lots of consistent love. Also, feed it treats. Become very aware of how you talk to yourself so that you are able to isolate unhelpful thoughts; look at their origin and reframe them if needed. I can categorically say that unless you master your mindset, you won't get very far in your business. So I implore you to take the time to take inventory of your mindset. Come back to this chapter often so you can nip Negative-Nelly thoughts in the bud, avoid burnout and enable mental growth.

Student Stories

"What I recently learned is to focus more on my journey instead of looking at the competitors' successful stores and feel like I would never be where they are now. I think the main lesson is to remember that if there is a market demand for their products, why would no-one buy from me? Even if I cannot commit so much time to my side-hustle, I learned what to focus on first and which decision makes a difference."

- Marta - Handmade Bosses Success Academy Student

WHAT ARE YOUR thoughts?

Chapter 4

BOUNTIFUL BOUNDARIES & GREAT GOALS

Do boundaries make you think of annoying neighbours, prying colleagues or unreasonable deadlines? You wouldn't be wrong. In this chapter we are going to be talking about boundaries and goals, two extremely important things to get right before starting your journey. One thing that many people forget when they commit to a project, social engagement or picking up grandma at the airport, is the opportunity cost. Basically, this means that with any opportunity you agree to, there will be a cost to you. This cost can be money, time, effort or anything you will need to ultimately give up in order to achieve a goal, go forward with a project or agree to do. Goals and boundaries are intertwined, without boundaries you won't achieve a goal.
An obvious example of this is that you'll have to spend money to get a graphic designer to help with your logo, so you are "losing" say, £350 to get a logo designed, easy-peasy.

However, a less obvious opportunity cost is when you are losing something that cannot be defined with a number. Let's say you agree to bake cakes for your niece's birthday party. Everyone loves your vanilla swirl cupcakes, and your sister has been bugging you for weeks to agree to make them; eventually you say yes. Seems innocent enough, right? Well, actually no. By agreeing to make these cakes,

Space for your notes

you're actually giving up a large chunk of your time. Time that would have otherwise been spent working towards a goal that means a great deal to you, say, working on your business. I'm not saying be a grouch with a capital G, but I am saying to be more aware of opportunity cost. In this instance, it's time, and you can't get back time.

Why is this so important? Well, a successful business owner does whatever they can to protect their time, effort and sometimes money. It's nothing against your Aunt Margaret, your neighbour Gary, or your friend Olivia, it's more to do with being protective over something that means a lot to you. If you need it defined another way, it's the ultimate act of self-love.

Coaching Questions:

What are some things you have agreed to, that you've later regretted?

Who is the usual culprit?

What could you have done with this time instead?

So why am I telling you this? Well, one of the best ways to lessen these awkward encounters and to help lessen the extent of opportunity cost, is to recognise that we will need to enforce boundaries on our handmade business journey. In fact, I encourage you to make up a whole rulebook of boundaries. This is important because of something called "decision fatigue". Decision fatigue can be best described using doughnuts. No, really.

Let's say you are trying to cut down your sugar intake, and at the beginning of the day you proudly say "No" to the offers of pastries and cookies. Go you. However, when you come toward the end of the day, you've used up all of your decision-making energy, and you're more likely to give in to temptation - bring on those doughnuts! So, by enforcing boundaries, and having a certain set of rules for yourself, you reduce decision fatigue, you're less likely to end up saying yes to something you will later regret.

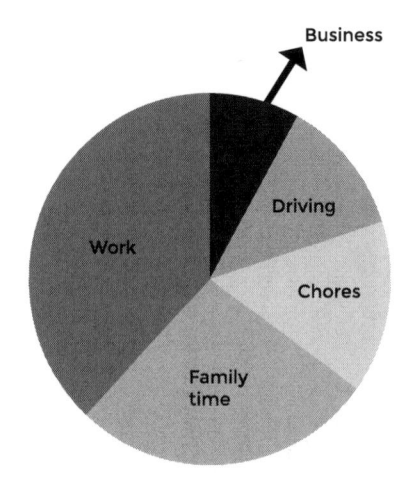

Coaching Questions:

Where are you spending the majority of your time? Try thinking of these categories:

- Business
- Relaxing
- Health/fitness
- Job/work
- Chores/errands
- Family time
- Friends
- Travelling

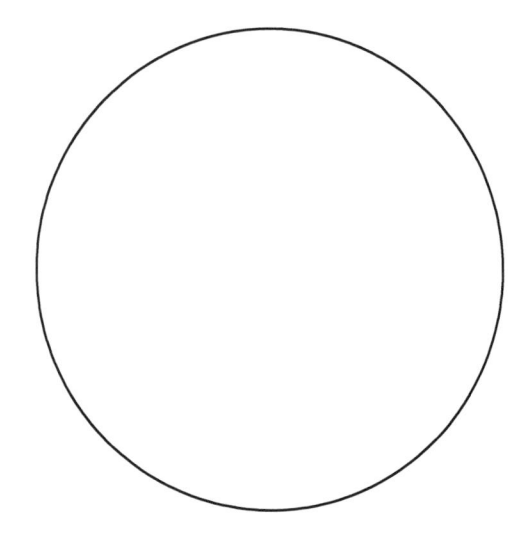

How do you want your time to be split instead?

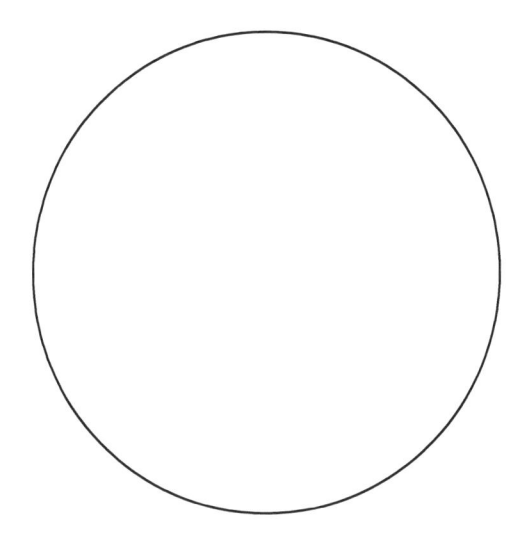

"What does this have to do with starting a handmade business Steph?" I can hear you asking. Well, quite a lot actually. There will be a lot of distractions, possible bad decisions and errors you will make along the way. We can reduce them by enforcing some hefty boundaries. Often, I will get messages from people who say "Steph, I just can't seem to find time to work on my business, I just don't know how I will ever be able to reach my goal if I don't have the time." To this, I usually answer with something like "Hey Boss, you seem to have a priorities and boundary problem, not a time problem."

Before you close this book and come to the conclusion that I'm a complete jerk, let me paint you a picture.

Jessie is at the very beginning of her handmade business journey. She works part-time at a local office supplies company, and looks after her two children on the days she's not working. She is known as a pinnacle of her community, she is always checking in on neighbours, getting their mail and bringing their bins in for them. Absolute legend you are Jessie. However, she has this dream of opening an online business where she sells her art, the passion that lights her up. She has only just started but has tons of ideas of paintings she would like to do next; she's filled up a whole list of iPhone notes with them. The downside is Jessie never gets round to it. By the time she's finished her chores, cooked dinner, cleaned, bathed the kids, run the Hoover round and picked up toys, she has one hour of peace and quiet before she passes out from exhaustion on the couch watching Netflix.

If I were Jessie, I would start by getting comfortable with the word "no". If her painting business means that much to her, she needs to carve out some time, set some boundaries and start working on this dream of hers.

No to getting Fred's mail. No to bringing in next-door's bin. No to writing a speech for the church event. No to cleaning up every night after dinner (it takes two to make a mess of the kitchen, right?) No, No and more No.

Listen, I'm not saying Jessie has to be an epic hard-ass to achieve this, but if her loved ones really valued her, a flat "I'm sorry, but I've set aside time to work on my dream business that day, I'm sure someone else would love the opportunity to help" is all it takes. This can actually be an example of a great boundary. Here are some more examples of personal rules and boundaries:

- You don't answer the phone to your friend between 7pm-9pm
- You say "no" to extra-curricular responsibilities
- You ask your child to allow you some focused work time,

and if they comply, you'll give them an epic amount of attention and playtime later
- You ask your partner to cook dinner three nights a week
- You ask your mum to collect grandma from the airport
- You refuse to engage in gossip and low-level conversation, as it drains you and leaves you feeling down
- You get your car washed, instead of spending three hours doing it yourself
- You outsource gardening, instead of trying to get the lawnmower to start for 20 minutes straight
- You ask your kids to unload the dishwasher in exchange for some extra pocket money
- You don't accept more than two invitations out a week.

Although many of these seem extreme, sometimes without realising it, we can get sucked into things we really don't enjoy. When I asked some Bosses in the community, 54% of them said they spend more than six hours a week doing things they had opted into, yet hate doing. Why? Because we don't want to disappoint people, we don't want to be disliked and we want approval. But this often comes at the cost of disappointing ourselves, which is not okay.

At the end of the day, we need to become good stewards of our time and energy to enable us to make room for a handmade business that has the capacity to grow and thrive. What personal boundaries do you need to enforce?

Coaching Questions:

Try asking yourself these questions:

1. Where do I spend my time on a week-by-week basis?

2. What weekly activities do I not enjoy?

3. Can I outsource some of these or refuse to do them?

4. Can I get this off my plate altogether?

5.   Am I doing this out of obligation or guilt?

6.   Is there a quicker or more efficient way of doing these things?

7.   What drains my energy weekly?

8.   How can I do less of those things?

9.   What energises me weekly?

10. How can I do more of those things?

If you still need more convincing Boss, I gotcha. Let's look at this as a numerical value. This is an exercise I encourage you to do every quarter, so you gradually start to understand where your time is best spent.

1.   How much do you plan on "paying yourself" from your business? £10 an hour? £1000 a month? £300 a week? Put a number on a segment of time, whatever it is.

2.   Work that out on an hour-by-hour basis; in this example, let's use £10 an hour.

3. What would you outsource, eliminate or automate for that amount each hour?

4. Do it!

EXAMPLE:

You hate clearing up the leaves in the garden. They're sticky, wet and you just never know what brown stuff is hiding under there…

You realise that this is a real low-level activity that you can outsource. You pop an ad up on the local community group and ask if anyone is interested in raking leaves for 1 hour a week at £8 an hour. Immediately you get a local teen interested and get that task off your plate. Voilà! You can now spend that hour creating new products or unwinding after a hard day of working on your business. Boss mode activated.

Where are you able to outsource some yucky tasks and "buy back" your time? In the beginning you may not have the ability to outsource much, but instead, you could automate it, delegate it or eliminate it altogether (do you really need to iron underwear???)

Coaching Questions:

How much will you pay yourself in your business every hour?

What can you outsource?

What can you eliminate?

What can you delegate and to who?

This leads me nicely onto the second part of this chapter: goals. This is where things start to get exciting.

Setting a goal for our business is like setting our destination on our satnav; it tells us when we're getting close to our original goal, when it's time to buckle down and work a bit harder, or when it's time to bring out the bubbly. Many new bosses don't set goals for their business, and it leaves them feeling a bit glum when they look to others for comparison and validation that what they've achieved is the "right" thing... which is probably the worst thing you can do.

Now we want to set goals for your business. This should be a numerical goal that stretches you, but doesn't leave you rocking back and forth in the corner of the room.

So what's your goal, Boss? What do you want to achieve with your business? Don't procrastinate on this task, and don't set vague goals like "I want to be happy". Nope, we want strong numerical goals that scream confidence. In fact, I'd love to bump into you on the street and say, "Quick, what's your goal?" and for you to shout, "£1000 a month!" for example.

I encourage you to get a bit more focused on your "why". Have you ever tried to save up for something as a kid, and you did whatever you could to get to your goal? You worked odd jobs, did chores, sold toys and helped out around the house. When you finally reached your goal, it felt so much sweeter because you had worked hard for it, and the journey was even more fun than the destination. In contrast, what about when people just told you to "save your money". It all felt a bit... boring, right? There was nothing to save FOR. The same can be said for your big Why. Yes, you want more money (obvs!) and there's nothing wrong with that. But WHY do you want more money? What will you use it for? How will you use it? Who for?

If you're struggling to think of a number, or you have one but you're not sure what the "right" answer is (newsflash: there isn't one) then think of what you would like to afford with your craft business. Think of it as your personal invoice to your business as what it will take for it to be run by you.

EXAMPLE:

To run this new business selling handmade organic skincare, I will need to be compensated with:

- a haircut every 4 weeks
- childcare for my toddler
- those jeans I wanted
- an extra family holiday every year
- the down payment on a new car
- a massage once a month
- a solo cinema trip each week

Then, put a numerical monthly or one-off value next to each of them:

I Deserve:	£ Monthly	£ One-Off
a haircut every 4 weeks £40	40	
childcare for my toddler £300	300.00	
those jeans I wanted £45 one-off		45.00
an extra family holiday every year £100	100	
down payment on a new car £500 one-off		500
a massage once a month £65	65	
a solo cinema trip each week £40	160	
Total	**£665.00**	**£545.00**

Lastly, add those up and write that number down.

£665 a month recurring

£545 one-off

That's how much your business needs to be able to pay you for you to sit at the head table as the CEO, founder and creator.

Just to be clear, I don't expect that you will begin making that amount straight away, however it may take a while to build up the business to the point where it makes that amount. I would also write that down as an "invoice due" date:

- £665 a month recurring
- £545 one-off
- Due in 6 months

This actually makes it easier for you to look at your Why and visualise exactly what you'll be using this revenue for. It makes us work that little bit harder if we know that we have a treat waiting for us when we achieve our goal!

Coaching Questions:

What's your big Why?

What will you use the extra money for?

What's your numerical goal?

When do you want to achieve it?

Now you have set these goals, it's time to go about actually achieving them. Yep, this may seem super-overwhelming, but in reality, it's as simple as just starting as soon as possible, even if it's just a small action. This will largely depend on you and your mindset (feel free to revisit the chapter on mindset!)

CHAPTER 4 : GOALS AND BOUNDARIES

There are some little tricks to help you be more likely to achieve your goals.

REVERSE-ENGINEER YOUR GOALS.

OK Boss, you have this mammoth goal that you've set for yourself, and it's making you sweat more than someone about to propose to someone on the first date. Your head is filled with scary thoughts of "How can I even achieve this?" or "That means I'll have to do something hard!"

I get it. But what if I told you it really doesn't have to be that hard? What if I told you that something little each day would compound and stack up to this big hairy-scary goal you set for yourself?

May I now introduce, reverse-engineering your goals. Take a look at the blank timeline below. At the far right-hand side, write the big goal you've set above, then at the far left, write today's date.

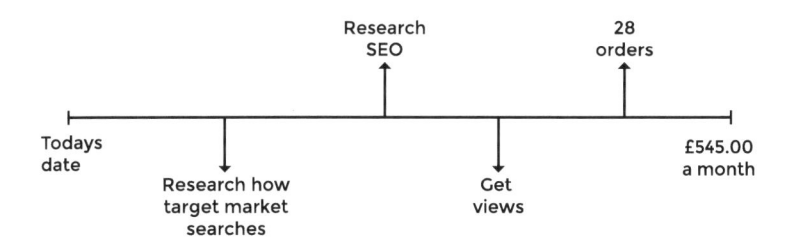

```
                    Research              28
                     SEO                orders
                      ↑                   ↑
    ├──────────┼──────────┼──────────┼──────────┤
  Todays                                    £545.00
   date           ↓              ↓          a month
              Research how      Get
              target market    views
                searches
```

Once you have done this, think about the steps that would get you to that goal in reverse order. In this example, to earn £545 a month from our business, we will have to get 28 orders (based on an average order value of £20). To get 28

79

orders, we will have to make sure our shop is getting views. To get views we need to make sure people are finding us through the search bar. To do that, we need to make sure our keywords are working for us. To do that, we need to research how our target market searches for our product on the platform we are using (in this example, let's use Etsy).

You can see that by doing this, not only do we make the goal less scary, but we also break it down into manageable steps. After filling in this timeline from today's date to your goal date, essentially you have a list of "to-dos" running from now until the time you reach that goal. Now, in order of time, write these below your timeline:

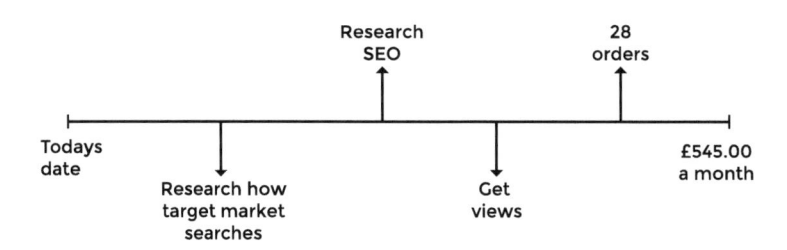

```
Todays                  Research              28
date                    SEO                   orders
  |                       ↑                    ↑                    £545.00
  |———————|———————|———————|———————|———————|————  a month
           ↓                       ↓
        Research how            Get
        target market           views
        searches
```

- Research target market
- Research SEO
- Get views
- 28 orders

There you have it: a list of to-do's for your business. You can chunk these down even more if it makes you feel better, for example:

- Research target market
  - Look at facebook group
  - Engage with followers
  - Ask question
- Research SEO
  - Watch handmade bosses youtube channel
  - Research & reasons to purchase

This then gives you day-by-day things to do to achieve that mini-goal.

Add Your Own Steps here:

Coaching Questions:

What are some things you need to achieve in order to attain your big goal in the time frame you have given yourself?

What are some smaller tasks you need to do to achieve those things?

Note: this may change depending on the social media platform you choose to use, but theoretically speaking, they should stay pretty much the same.

If these tasks are looking pathetically small - good! Start with those first and begin to build momentum through achieving the smaller tasks first. If you have ever started by cleaning the sink, and then two hours later ended up clearing out the cupboards, tidying the cutlery and doing the washing, then you know what I mean by this!

On the other hand, don't feel bad if you still feel overwhelmed; as mentioned before, this is a learning curve and we aren't all born with the know-how of how to do this, that's why I'm here supporting you through the journey - you got this!

VISUALISE THE END POINT

This is an exercise that may border on the "woo-woo", but if you have a goal that brings butterflies to your tummy, makes you smile and gets your motor running (and your goals should!) then it's a great idea to visualise the outcome frequently. There will be ups and downs along the way, some days you may even question whether your goal is worth it, but making sure that you regularly visualise the end point will reinforce this goal, and push you through those down times.

Coaching Questions:

When you visualise your goal, answer some of these questions:

1.   What will my life look like when I achieve this goal?

2.   What will I look like?

3. What will my home look like?

4. How will I feel?

5. What will it mean for my family and loved ones?

6. What kind of job will I be doing?

7.   Will I be doing it alone?

Another great way to visualise is using dream boards. I've used them since 2014 and I'm not kidding when I say 80% of what I put on there eventually comes true. If you watch my weekly live videos in the Facebook group, you'll see there is always a dream board behind me. Printing off images and words that will represent your life when you achieve your goal and placing them in a collage where you can see them daily, will be a good reminder to yourself not to sweat the small stuff, and keep yourself pushing toward your goal. There are digital online collage makers too, such as Pinterest and Canva that will make this process super easy. I've left a space for you to plan your dream board in this book too, so everything is easily accessible in one place.

Coaching Questions:

Plan your own dream board over the next couple of pages:

CHAPTER 4 : GOALS AND BOUNDARIES

SHARE WITH FRIENDS

Sharing is caring! If the idea of sharing your goals with your loved ones seems scary, that could be your comfort zone trying to call you back into its lair, and a sign that you don't have faith in your ability to complete it. Share your goals with a trusted friend, as well as the date by which you want to complete them, and keep each other accountable. After all, we have New Year's resolutions right? No-one is a stranger to goals.

Coaching Questions:

Who can I share my big goal with?

TRACK PROGRESS

If your goal is one attached to a number, it's a fun exercise to track it somewhere visually. A bit like ticking off the days before a big vacation on a calendar builds excitement, crossing off milestones to your goal will build momentum and keep you moving toward it.

£1000.00

£500.00

£0

CHAPTER 4 : GOALS AND BOUNDARIES

Coaching Questions:

How will I track my progress?

Doodle, draw or write your progress tracker below:

CELEBRATE SMALL WINS

We don't celebrate ourselves nearly as much as we should. Went to the gym even though you didn't want to? Celebrate! Posted one new listing when it all felt a bit daunting? Winner! Made two sales this month? You're killing it! We often focus too much on the negative, instead of reframing it as a good thing. Let's say you got two sales in the past 30 days. It would be so easy to say "Ergh, only two? It's not working, I'm probably being really stupid and rubbish."

This is not a healthy mindset, and actually something that will catapult you into the sabotaging business loop pattern faster than you can say "broken dream." Instead, let's actually take a hot minute to celebrate the fact that you convinced two complete strangers to purchase from you. They valued your product so much that they went and got their credit card, typed in the information and pressed the order button. Now you know people like what you have to sell, it's just a case of scaling. That's the easy part.

See how that's different? Mark the occasion by writing a list of small and large celebrations that you will commit to when you hit your goals. Here are some ideas to get you started:

- Take yourself to your fav walking spot
- Go for a manicure
- Do 30 minutes of yoga
- Treat yourself to a new book
- Meditate
- Buy yourself your favourite tea

Coaching Questions:

What have been some wins for you over the last six months? List the big and small ones.

How did you celebrate these previously?

How will you celebrate future wins?

KEEP A WIN TRACKER

Sometimes we forget how far we have come, on days when everything seems against us. Write a win tracker and write down every weekly win, however big or small. This especially helps keep imposter syndrome at bay.

Coaching Questions:

Track your wins below:

WRITE YOUR BIG GOAL DOWN DAILY

Studies have shown that writing your goals down frequently means that your 1.2x more likely to achieve them. Knowing this, I hope you'll go and grab that pen and paper and keep it handy! During these studies, it was found that writing these goals meant that your brain actually "stored" them for longer, and embedded it into your brain so much, that you start to begin to find ways to make them happen. The same can be said for visualisation too, basically, anything you can do to embed this into your conscious and subconscious brain - do it.

Student Stories

"I have worked with Steph both on a 121 basis and inside the HBSA course for over nine months now. Not only have my Etsy shop sales, stats and revenue grown tremendously, so has my confidence, resulting in my ability to believe in myself and design work more, work with my ideal clients, raise my prices and build a consistent and blossoming business.
A big thank you to Steph and the team"

- Meghan from BrandKynd.

Chapter 5

THE PERFECT BUSINESS NAME IN 24 HOURS

Choosing your business name is something that so many bosses get caught up on, and for good reason too. It's when everything becomes real, and your business ideas begin to become reality. However, so many people procrasti-name for weeks, or even months. It makes sense that the first "real" aspect of your business coming to life requires some deep thinking and a sense of "getting it right". But so many people get caught up on the "shoulds" when it comes to their business name. I estimate a sizeable chunk of businesses make the naming process so hard, that they end up never getting past this first "hurdle" in business.

You may be saying:

- "I can't start my business until I have a good name"
- "I have a business idea, but no name"
- "No-one will buy from a business with a rubbish name"

These are just some of the posts I see in our Facebook community each week. The reality is though, there are plenty of times in history when a business with a perceived "terrible name", has succeeded, and even gone on to become a multi-million company.

Space for your notes

Let's take Apple: apples have nothing to do with what they sell. It's simple for sure, but if you'd never heard of them, you'd think they made cider instead of technology.

What about Tiffany's? That brings to mind a beauty salon or a local burger joint to me, rather than a top-of-the range jewellery company.

You'll see there are tons of examples of businesses like these, so honestly, you don't have to spend a bucket-load of time stuck on the name. Let's be real: whatever your business name is, you'll more than likely have to explain it to people anyway - so avoid the drama and relax - your brand values are a hundred times more important than your name (more on that later).

My challenge for you is to come up with your name in a day. Yep, a day. That's plenty enough time to find a name that works for you, and remember, you can always rebrand and rename later on if you want to - no biggie (just look at Facebook becoming Meta!) Coming next you will find some handy ways to come up with your name, and some things to think about before you decide on what your business will ultimately be called. (You can find a great video on choosing your business name in the Book Bonus Resources that can be found here: www.handmadebosses.com/bookbonus).

The process we follow when I'm working with a new business owner 1-1 is that we will begin with brainstorming words and phrases (I'll shortly explain what sorts of things to write down). We then make a shortlist of names (no more than five) and then eventually we will pick the final name.

HOW TO BRAINSTORM NAME IDEAS IN 24 HOURS OR LESS

SECTION 1 - THE WORDS AND PHRASES BRAINSTORM

1. **Use related words in different ways.** When you describe what you can create, how do you do it? There are usually several words you can use to describe the same thing or feeling, so making a note of these first will be a great exercise to do. For example, let's say you make handmade soaps. What words come to mind when you think of soaps? We could say clean, squeaky clean, bubbles, suds, relax, refresh and so on. We are basically expanding our frame of mind around what we sell, and thinking of different vocabulary ideas.

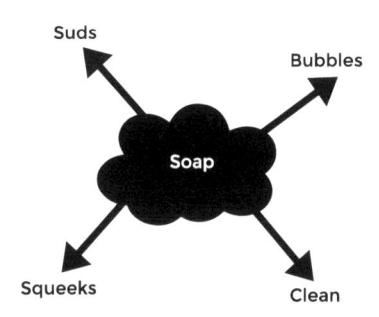

Diagram: Soap cloud with arrows pointing to Suds, Bubbles, Squeeks, Clean.

2. **Try using a thesaurus.** Using a thesaurus can add another layer to the above process. For example, when we type "crochet" into a free online thesaurus tool (Google for these) you will get: bind, fasten, mend, sew, unite, weave, just to name a few. For our soap example, detergent and soapsuds. Not a great list, but If I plug in the word "clean" instead, we get, blank, bright, clear, elegant, fresh, immaculate, and many more. Combine these with the words we had in the previous task.

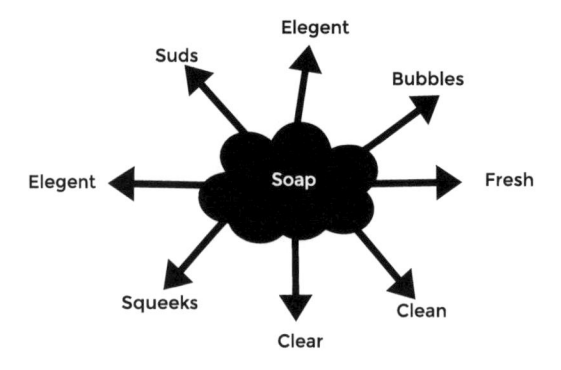

```
              Elegent
       Suds     ↑
        ↖       |     Bubbles
                      ↗
Elegent ← [ Soap ] → Fresh
        ↙       |     ↘
     Squeeks    ↓    Clean
              Clear
```

3. **Try a different language.** Again, if you want to add another layer to this, try investigating the name of what you want to sell in a different language. Some examples of "jewellery" in other languages are: nakit, juwelen, bijoux, joyería and many more. In our running example of "soap" you have; sapun, savon, seife, sapone, and sabonete, to name a few. Add some of these to your brainstorm too and by now you should a big ol' brainstorm collection of words and phrases.

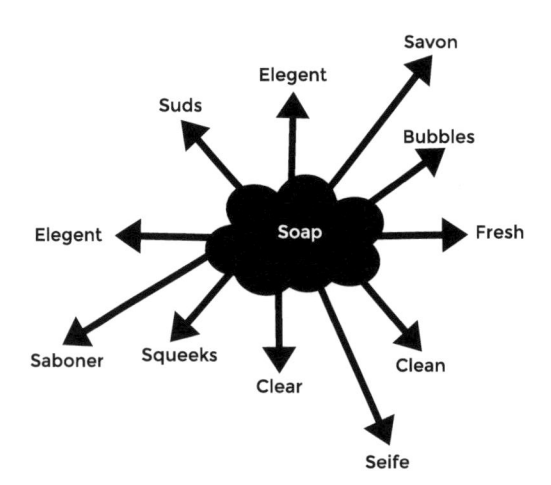

```
                         Savon
                          ↗
              Elegent
       Suds     ↑
        ↖       |     Bubbles
                      ↗
Elegent ← [ Soap ] → Fresh
        ↙       |     ↘
Saboner Squeeks ↓    Clean
              Clear    ↘
                      Seife
```

4. **Add adjectives.** What we effectively have right now, is words on a page (duh!) You could start to combine them and already begin seeing some possible business

CHAPTER 5 : THE PERFECT BUSINESS NAME IN 24 HOURS

names (if so write these down separately) but let's start to add some adjectives to spice up our brainstorm a little. Start to write down some words that you'd love people to describe your work as. You can begin simply by using words like "good" or "right" but try and go a bit deeper. Some ideas to get you started are: great, first, new, right, different, important, fantastic, beautiful etc. Then take some of these and use a free online thesaurus tool to get some other words for them. So let's say "beautiful" really tickles your fancy; our thesaurus tells us some other words for this are: charming, alluring, appealing, cute, dazzling, delicate, elegant, exquisite etc. Add as many of these as you like to your brainstorm (don't worry, brainstorms are meant to be messy!)

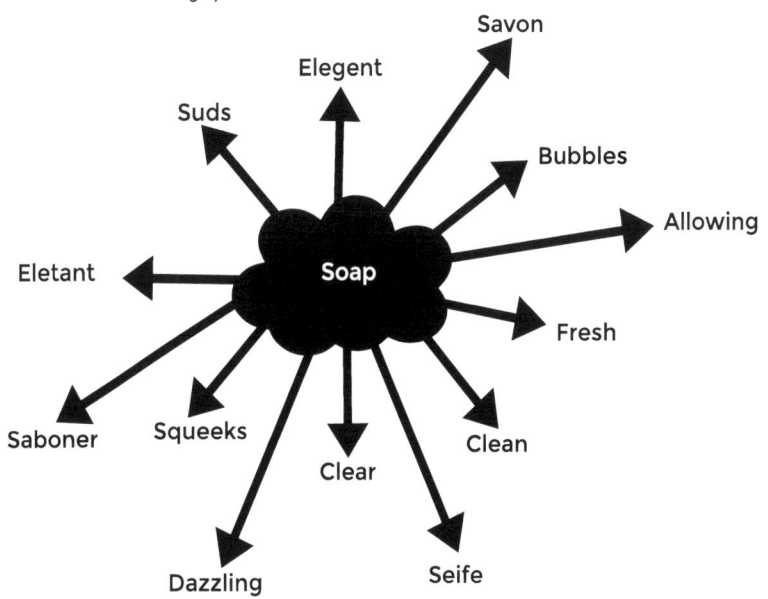

Brainstorm around the word **Soap** with branches to: Savon, Elegent, Suds, Bubbles, Allowing, Fresh, Clean, Seife, Clear, Dazzling, Squeeks, Saboner, Eletant.

Coaching Questions:

Add your own name brainstorm here:

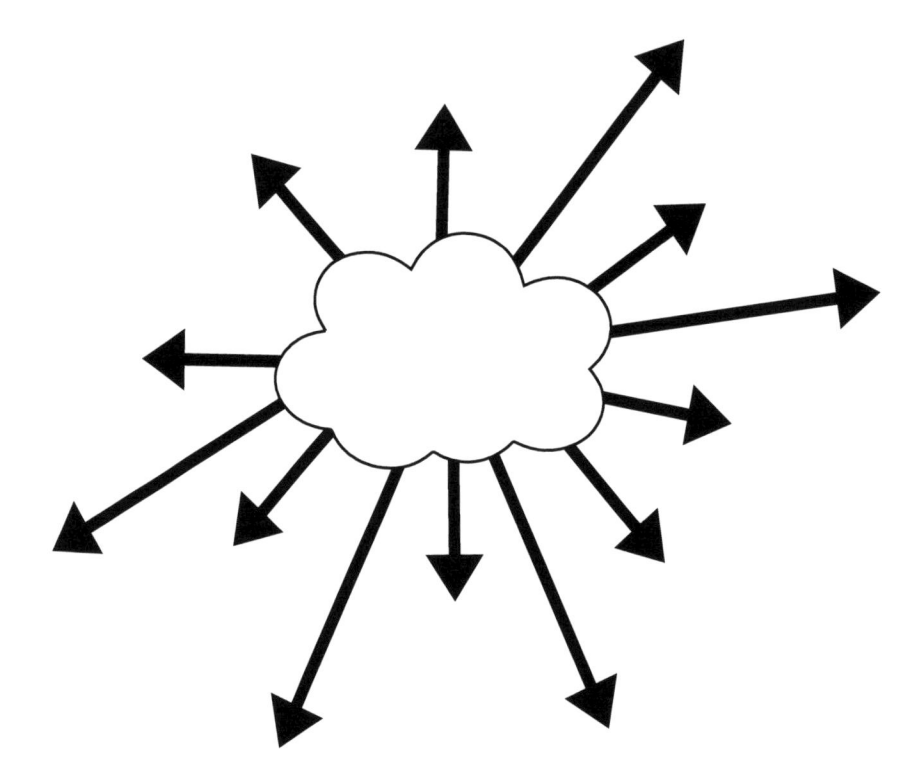

SECTION 2 - THE COMBINATIONS AND SHORTLIST

At this stage, we have probably 50+ words we can play with to create our name. There are a few ways we can do this, but the most effective way of doing this is to use wordplay and combos (or both).

1. **Combinations.** Look at your words from your brainstorm and start to combine them wherever they make sense. For example, taking the words "fresh" and "bubbles" and combining them into "fresh bubbles" or "alluring clean", "elegant suds", "dazzling savon", "fresh, clean and clear" etc. Write down whichever ones roll off the tongue.

2. **Use wordplay.** Take your favourite words from your brainstorm and find rhyming words, alliterations, slang or puns that would add some pizazz to your name. For example, finding words that rhyme with soap: dope, cope, scope and hope. Or alliterations such as: soaky, soapy and soulful. Just from these two forms of wordplay, we have some great possible combos, "dope soap", "hope soap", "soaky soap", "soulful soap" and "soaky soulful soap" etc. Write down the ones that really hit different for you.

3. **Shortlist the sucker.** Okay Boss, you now have some absolutely banging word combos - look at you, secret wordsmith! Now it's time to shortlist those into the ones you like. We really only want a maximum of five.

Coaching Questions:

What are five possible shortlisted names?

Things to note before deciding on a final name.

Now you have a shortlist of five possible names, it's time to wheedle them down to ONE with these considerations:

1. **Make sure to check the legalities.** If you are in the UK, check Companies House or your local authorities to check if the name is already taken. You can also add a Google search to the mix to make sure that someone else hasn't taken your name already. The other reason to do this is to make sure that prospective customers won't confuse someone else's business with yours when looking online for your brand specifically.

2. **Don't limit what you can sell with your name.** If you ever plan on expanding the business, take this into consideration when naming your business. If you want to sell wax melts and reed diffusers one day, don't name

your business "Randall's Candles" as this will cause confusion with potential customers thinking you just sell candles.

3. **Make sure it relates to your brand values.** Your brand will be known for certain values that attract your dream customer. Although we haven't covered that quite yet in this book, you don't want to repel your target audience straight out of the gate. If being eco-friendly is important to you, then maybe bake that right into the business name, so that value of yours is directly communicated.

4. **Get catchy.** Probably not much explaining needed here, but the more catchy the name, the better.

5. **Simplicity is key.** If in doubt, go simple. People have a tendency to over-complicate names and make them very long, when in reality, people won't remember a name that's more than four words long.

6. **Avoid using your own name,** unless you want to build a personal brand. This is my pet peeve for sure. It keeps your business a bit stuck, and makes it difficult to scale. Let's say you're starting a painting business that is called "Art by Andrea". That's great, but if ever you want to outsource some part of your business, then people will expect only Andrea to do it. Or let's say you make jewellery and your business name is "Jewellery made by Julia". Again, if you have any hope of scaling your business, you don't want to be forever involved in every single aspect of your creation process, because people will be expecting Julia to make it.

7. **Make sure the domain is available.** Lastly, go onto a domain service where you can check to see if it's possible to purchase the domain name for your business. I would 100% recommend doing this even if you have no intention of using it for your own website yet.

Coaching Questions:

What is your final business name?

Chapter 6

LOVELY LEGALITIES

The legal bits behind any business always look super scary and something that you'd rather put away, go chill out on the couch and watch movies for four hours whilst consuming your body weight in chocolate. However, despite me agreeing with you about legalities being a solid #1 on the "excitement scale" it's something we all have to deal with. You don't want to risk starting your business on shaky foundations and risk fines, closure and even imprisonment.

Disclaimer

I am not a legal or finance expert and the information in this chapter is given purely as a rough idea of where to start. Please be sure to check your current and local rules and regulations, and be aware some given in this book may be out of date.

TAXES AND ACCOUNTS

First out of the gate is taxes and accounts. The best attitude to have with this side of things is "keep a record of everything". Begin by deciding how you will track your transactions in and out of your business. I would recommend a basic spreadsheet like the one pictured in the following pages below, and updating it every day or every week.

The best part about doing your own accounts, is that you can have a "bird's eye view" of how your business is performing financially at any time, whereas if you hire an accountant, there may be more delay to finding out this info. This is why I would recommend adding an extra layer to this, by adding in some more financial fields to your tracking spreadsheet:

Income + Expenses Tracker

Month:

Income:

Date	Order Ref	Income

Outgoings

Date	Order Ref	Income

Starting Balance
Monthly Income
_____
Monthly Expenses
Difference (+ or -)

The big benefit of doing this is you will understand how much tax you may have to pay straight away.

For example, let's say that you see your income is £20,000. Subtract your allowable expenses of £5,000, that leaves a taxable profit of £15,000. After checking your personal allowance (or tax limit) you find out that you can earn £13,500 before paying any tax. That means that you have a taxable income of £1500. Easy, right?

From then you can see that the current income tax rate is 20%, so that means your tax bill is 20% of £1500, which totals £300. This is a purely theoretical example, but it really enables you to have a rough estimate of your tax bill in plenty of time before it needs to be paid. You can even build this as a formula into your spreadsheet and have the wonders of technology work it out for you.

Coaching Questions:

Track your own income and expenses in the next few pages:

Income + Expenses Tracker

Month:

Income:

Outgoings

Date	Order Ref	Income

Date	Order Ref	Income

Starting Balance
Monthly Income

___

Monthly Expenses
Difference (+ or -)

Income + Expenses Tracker

Month:

Income: Outgoings

Date	Order Ref	Income

Date	Order Ref	Income

Starting Balance
Monthly Income

Monthly Expenses
Difference (+ or -)

Transaction logging is also a big part of accounts, and I would recommend logging your transactions fully, at least until you find your groove with accounting. You can use an automatic software, or use a spreadsheet too.

Coaching Questions:

How will I track my transactions?

Make sure to keep receipts, invoices and paperwork relating to a business transaction, and be sure to keep business transactions separate from personal ones (this is a lot easier with a separate business bank account). It also makes it look a ton more professional when making payments through a proper business name. This may differ slightly, depending on how you form your business/company.

Coaching Questions:

How will I ensure receipts and invoices are kept safe and organised?

COMPANY FORMAT

This is essentially how your business is viewed for tax purposes and differs depending on where you are geographically, but usually there are a couple of obvious ways to do this. You can be a sole trader (trading as yourself, by yourself) or you can be a limited company (trading as a separate company entity, usually your business name.) Each has its pros and cons, such as more privacy protection, asset protection and easier accounts. I would recommend speaking to a professional to find out which one is right for you.

Coaching Questions:

What company format will I use?

SELLING REGULATIONS

When selling products, you need to make sure that you educate yourself about some laws surrounding the products being sold. Vaguely speaking, you have to make sure that the description is not misleading, it matches that description, it's fit for purpose and of satisfactory quality (Sale of Goods Act 1979). To check if you comply, start your search with tradingstandards.uk (if you are in the UK) or the Federal Trade Commission (if you are in the USA).

With trading online, you will need to provide your personal

details such as name, address and cancellation rights, to name a few. If you're selling on a marketplace like Etsy, you may receive help with this.

Coaching Questions:

Selling regulation notes:

PRODUCT REGULATIONS

There are certain safety regulations when dealing with things like toys and clothes. Some products will need extra certification or certain markings to ensure they comply with regulations. One example of this is CE marks on toys. If you want to check if your products meet standards, start your search by looking on websites such as Trading Standards (tradingstandards.uk) if you are in the UK, or similar bodies depending on where you live.

Coaching Questions:

Product regulation notes:

GDPR

GDPR (affectionately known as the General Data Protection Regulation) came into effect May 2016 and gives consumer and the general public more say and rights over how companies control and process their data. There are other versions of this in different countries, but you may be required to write a privacy policy, and/or other supporting documents. Check out your local governing body for details.

Coaching Questions:

GDPR notes:

COPYRIGHT

Some original works can fall under the legality of copyright. Some things cannot be copyrighted, but many "created works" such as books, images, music etc. can be. I'm not a copyright expert but make sure to do your due diligence and research copyright laws in your country.

Coaching Questions:

Copyright notes:

INSURANCES

Just as you would insure your home, you may also wish to insure your business too. Costs in legal battles can get out of control quickly, and being sure to insure yourself against them is a great thing to do; it may also be a legal requirement depending on where you live. Here are some things to think about when it comes to insurance (again, I'm not a legal or insurance expert and it's up to you to make sure you have the correct insurances in place!)

PUBLIC LIABILITY

This covers any damage or injuries whilst a member of the public is interacting with your business, or through any business activities, for example if someone trips over your table and hurts themself at an event.

PRODUCT LIABILITY

This is an insurance that covers claims or legal costs if someone is injured, or their property is damaged by a product you have sold.

THINGS TO NOTE:

Something else you may need to be aware of is making sure your home insurer is advised you are running a business from home. Failing to do so may invalidate or cancel your policy.

SHOWS, CRAFTS FAIRS AND IN-PERSON EXHIBITING

Some locations will not allow you to exhibit unless you have a certain type of insurance, or certain amount of cover (like £2,000,000 for example).

READ THE FINE PRINT!

Make sure that you understand what is and isn't included in a policy before you take it out. Some may have excesses and exclusions so it's always best to be aware of these.

Coaching Questions:

Insurance notes:

WHAT ARE YOUR *thoughts?*

Chapter 7

WONDERING WHERE TO SELL?

Now we have all of the important basics out of the way, it's time to start to think about how we will launch our business, beginning with where to sell. There are two main types of places that I would recommend beginners to start with, these are online Marketplaces, and your own website, I would however only choose ONE. The reason for this (as you'll see, this will be a running theme in this book) is that too many budding bosses spread themselves too thinly with their time, energy and cash flow across too many things. Doing "all the things" and "hustle culture" is such a damaging attitude in our space, and is the main reason why businesses in our niche fail. (don't forget to download a list of my favourite places to sell in the Book Bonuses section at www.handmadebosses.com/bookbonus)

This is an important step in launching your business: it's vital to pick a platform that works for YOU. People will try and tell you to pick one or the other, but in reality, that may have been what worked for THEM, and their opinions will reflect that. I have done both, and each platform has different strengths and recommendations.

Ideally, you should pick a platform that enables you to start to gain traction quickly, and will enable you to grow into the vision you have for your business (see chapter on mindset).

If you get this right, you will only have to make this decision once, until you're ready to add another platform to your business repertoire.

Many handmade business owners struggle to get the early development of their business going because they choose the wrong platform to begin with, so be sure to spend some time thinking about this - quite literally the success of your business depends on it.

As I've mentioned, it's totally up to you where you begin to sell, but I have outlined some of the highlights of each option below, to help you make your decision.

MARKETPLACE

(for example, Etsy, Ebay, Amazon, Handmade etc.)

You get a ready-made traffic source. The main attraction of marketplaces is that they have spent millions cultivating a "ready-made" audience for your products. Places like Etsy (my favourite and one that I teach the vast majority of my students to start on) make it super easy to start getting sales easily. Think about it: if you were shopping for a handmade wedding tiara, you wouldn't necessarily go to Ebay or Amazon, but you would head to Etsy. Google would also encourage you to do the same thing by putting Etsy at the top of the search results. Try searching "handmade wedding tiara" and you'll see what I mean. I'll wait.

Because of this, Etsy has become the household name for handmade artisan products. This means that it has a ready-made audience of customers who are in the zone for buying, they are there to purchase a product - it's basically a ready-made traffic source for a huge audience for handmade products.

You get the trust factor. Let me pose you a question: if you were going to buy a lawnmower, where would you buy it from? An unknown website, or a marketplace with an easy, full money-back guarantee if it goes wrong, doesn't arrive or arrives damaged? Your customers will shop at online marketplaces for the same reason - they get that "know, like and trust" factor straight away. This is something that is very difficult to build with your own website (as I'll explain below).

They ease you into business. Whenever I personally coach a new handmade business start-up, I can see the path ahead of them. There will be high-highs and low-lows, with a smattering of dull days thrown in there too. At the beginning though, you are super susceptible to giving up early on. This is mainly because it's super easy to quit a new venture when the call of the comfort zone attracts you back to it like a magnet. Here's a phrase you will hear throughout this book: "Maker, make it easy!"

They get you set up quickly. If done right, opening a storefront on a marketplace should take you no more than 1-2 hours. Mainly this is because of their streamlined step-by-step processes, and "fill in the blank" areas - they've spent thousands researching and making the process simple.

Legal policies are easy. Depending on the marketplace, the legal documents may be "done for you" or not needed at all. Check with your desired marketplace to see what you need, and what you don't

Easy reporting tools. Again, marketplaces have spent a

pretty penny working out how their sellers interface with their stats, and so they make it effortless for you to find out what you need to. They even have hand-dandy downloads for things like your accounting, taxes and transaction history.

You get seller help. No-one likes the first time they get a negative review, feedback or criticism, but having a marketplace by your side makes the whole process a whole lot smoother. Yes, sometimes they have their quirky rules that may annoy you at times, but remember, protection is a two-way street, the customers wouldn't flock to that marketplace if they weren't protected.

Safe payments for customers. Following on from above, marketplaces have a boatload of encryptions and safety certificates when it comes to taking payments. Best thing is with many marketplaces, if there's a glitch with the customer's payments or credit cards, it's the marketplace's problem and not yours.

Easier integrations and tools. Many marketplaces have integrations that you can implement with the click of a button. Take Mailchimp (an email marketing software) as an example. This seamlessness "talks to Etsy within minutes, saving you time and effort" and Google's "integrations with X" to see what's available for your chosen marketplace.

There are a few marketplaces out there that are a great place to start. But are they worth the time and effort? Some I have signed up for have definitely not been worth it, with hours spent on it and £0 to show for it. But some have been worth every minute and penny. To avoid wasting your time, before signing up to them, ask yourself these questions:

- What are the reviews (Trustpilot, Google Reviews etc.) for this marketplace from sellers and customers?
- Have I seen this advertised anywhere?
- How are they getting customers to their platform?
- What calibre of sellers are also on the platform?
- Is there any market share information online about how popular they are with consumers?
- Is there historical evidence that people can do well with this marketplace?

Below is a list of marketplaces starting with my favourites, right down to ones I haven't personally used:

- Etsy
- NotOnTheHighStreet
- Amazon Handmade
- Ebay
- Folksy
- Numonday

Coaching Questions:

What are some Marketplaces that interest me?

Why?

YOUR OWN WEBSITE

If the idea of opening your own website makes you want to run to the pub and hide, don't fret! Having your own website is so much easier than it was ten years ago. You don't have to know coding or any complicated jargon any more, and there are a number of websites that make it super easy for you which I'll list later.

Let's go over some of the great points about having your own website:

You own the website. When you open up your own website, to a certain extent, you own everything about it. You own the domain, the home page, product pages - everything. It gives makers a greater sense of achievement, ownership and control. If a marketplace were to close down tomorrow (unlikely, but a possibility) then you will still own your website.

More customisation options. Further to the previous point, because you have more ownership of the website, you can customise it greatly. While this may be a headache for some people, for others it will be branding heaven (more on that later).

Fewer do's and don'ts. With any marketplace, there will be some house rules that you'll have to follow. Examples include dispatching a package on time and replacing damaged orders. With your own website, you will have less of these "rules" in place. Word of warning though: usually marketplaces have these rules for a reason, so not following these best practices on your own website may be a fast-track way to a few angry customers.

Less competition. When you search for a product on a marketplace, you are greeted with hundreds of options, most of which will be from your competition. However, when people come across your website, you will have their full undivided attention (hopefully) on your products only.

Less fees (probably). Many people flock to their own website when they start to tot up the fees (more on this later) however, the sad fact is that once they add up their own website fees (usually a monthly price) and payment processing fees (usually a % per transaction) it's not much different. Be sure to do your research on the fees before jumping in.

Lots of people love the idea of running their own website, but before you jump in, ask yourself these questions:

1. Do you have an audience to leverage for traffic? Social media audience for example.

2. Do you have the budget to potentially pay for ads to drive visits?

3. Do you have the time and know-how to use SEO and content to drive organic traffic to your website?

4. Do you have someone you can call or a helpdesk to contact if things go wrong or there's a glitch?

Below I've listed some great places to start to look if you are considering building your own website:

- Shopify (my fav)
- Wix
- Squarespace
- BigCommerce
- Magento
- Wordpress (for more advanced users)

Coaching Questions:

What website builders interest you?

Why?

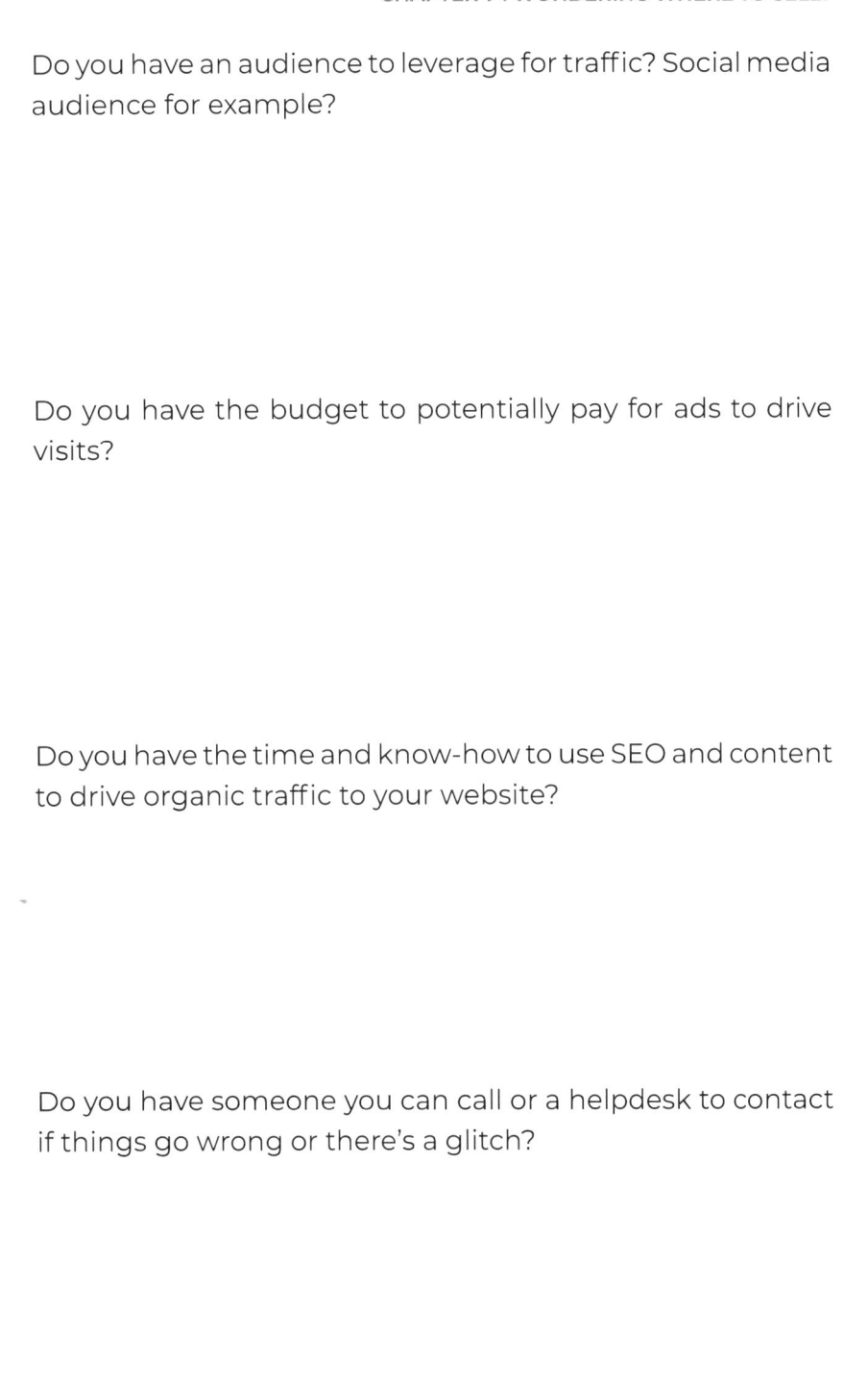

Do you have an audience to leverage for traffic? Social media audience for example?

Do you have the budget to potentially pay for ads to drive visits?

Do you have the time and know-how to use SEO and content to drive organic traffic to your website?

Do you have someone you can call or a helpdesk to contact if things go wrong or there's a glitch?

Whatever option you choose, make sure you stand 100% behind your decision. Changing your mind halfway through the process will only delay getting sales for longer! In my humble opinion, Etsy as a marketplace offers more strengths than any of the others, especially with their ready-made audience of people who want to buy your product on the platform.

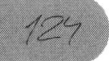

WHAT ARE YOUR *thoughts?*

Chapter 8

THE TERRIFICALLY TANTALISING TRIO: Target Market, Branding & Products

This is where things get ramped up, Boss, this is one of the most important chapters in this book, and one where I would recommend making detailed notes, and dog-earing pages for later. As I mentioned before - this book is yours - scrawl all over it, note-take in the margins and highlights things that are important!

These three things work as a trio, they work in unison to elevate your business, and effectively get more sales. These are markets, products and branding. Like a stool, it gets wobbly and falls over if one of these three legs are broken or missing.

Before diving into why these are so important, let's go over the trio (the three legs of the stool) first::

Space for your notes

TARGET MARKET

The ideal person that you have in mind when making your product, and who you will actively target your products toward.

PRODUCTS

The product that you make because of a certain pain point your target market has. The product should have a USP (unique selling point) that makes it stand out from competitors.

BRANDING

A brand that ties the two together and magnetically attracts the target customer. The brand should have a USP (unique selling point) that makes it stand out from competitors.

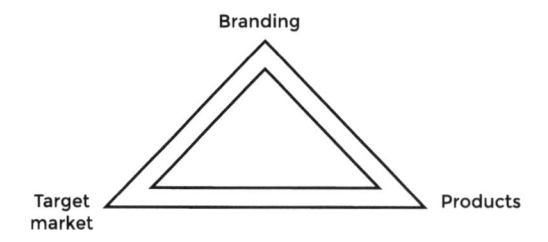

Think about what happens to a shop when one of these things is less than adequate. The best way to explain it is to use an example, so let's take a look at what happens when we saw off a stool leg:

EXAMPLE A

Jeff has a shop that sells wooden signs. He loves working with wood and remembers creating some signs with his grandfather when he was young. His shop is called Made For Dudes and has been in business for six months. He makes funny signs aimed at couples without children that have their own home. He knows that his target market loves humour, and he has found signs with swear words sell well for him, and make his audience laugh. He knows that women are his primary purchaser, but usually for gifts or to add pizazz to their home. His shop has a lot of dark green and black items, and he advertises in magazines aimed at a male audience. He is wondering why he has not grown as quickly as he hoped he would.

Problem: Branding + Target Market

Reason: Jeff's stats are quietly telling him that he has a branding issue. If Jeff's primary purchasers are females, then going for a less masculine and more neutral brand will stop "turning off" female customers that want to buy it for a gift. I would suggest Jeff pivots his brand to more neutral colours and a logo that will attract both male and female avatars. Alternatively, he may want to change the name from "made for dudes" as it gives the impression that "males" will only find his signs funny or amusing.

EXAMPLE B

Julia owns a general shop where she sews things out of fabric. Within her shop she has scrunchies, headbands, bandanas for dogs, collars, fat quarters and plastic bag holders. She sells mainly scrunchies but has found herself attracted to making "higher end" scrunchies for wedding days. She knows that her target market is women and young girls that want to make sure they look their best for an event. She has found that a lot of people like her items, but never actually purchase from her. When she does in-person events, people love her items, but online, it doesn't come across.

Problem: Product + Target Market (connection to target customer's pain point)

Reason: Julia's "generalised" shop and brand has made it hard for people to connect with it. Within her shop she has items for weddings, pets, crafters and homeware. I would advise that there are too many target markets. If she wants to carry on with scrunchies for special occasions, she needs to connect to the USP of that product - or make one!

Together, we come up with a new packaging idea to make the scrunchie more special, displaying it in a gift box (with a note and custom name printed on it) so it's more suitable for a wedding, and becomes more valuable to the target market. Sales go up as she has a unique product that has a specific USP which connects to the target customer's pain point - flower girls' styled hair stays in for two hours after the wedding ceremony as they jump around and play, so the parents need an easy way to spruce it up quickly.

EXAMPLE C

Grace has a business that sells a variety of different products. She sells candles, beeswax wraps, wallets, jewellery, keyrings, wooden bird-feeders, face masks, hair bows, printable art and handmade dog treats. She has had a few sales here and there, but is struggling to grow the business. She has no idea why and has tried all the things when it comes to marketing. She is ready to give up at this point.

Problem: Product, Target Market and Branding

Reason: Poor Grace has a lot of work to do, but alas, she is a human of many talents! Although she is super creative and has a great deal of different things she can make, I encourage her to pick one niche of products (one target market) to create and serve, as trying to serve everyone means she is serving no-one. She should start by only creating what she enjoys doing, and is profitable for her. Then she should start working on her target audience and her brand. This may require building her shop from the ground up again, but without the trio working for her, she's in trouble.

When my students finish the Handmade Bosses Success Academy, one of the many things we like to see is shops that have a strong and sturdy trio stool. As I look over their businesses whilst writing this, the most successful shops have:

- a clear niche target audience
- a target audience with a clear pain point (need)
- a product that obviously demonstrates and solves that need in a non-complicated way
- a product with a unique selling point that triumphs over the competition
- a product that has been reviewed and gets 95% glowing reviews
- a brand that attracts the perfect target demographic to their shop
- a clear and steady shopper journey

There are a lot more moving parts than just this short list, but having these down is like building a house on strong foundations vs building it on a cracked, shaky foundation prone to subsidence. Shops that build these foundations are those that quickly grow their business from zero to six figures in under 24 months. One of my students that sells handcrafted wooden trays, hit the 6-figure mark within ten months of starting his business. Another hit the 6-figure mark and paid off student debt, bought a second home and rented out the first.

THIS is the power of getting this right, it could damn well change your life!

Whenever I speak to handmade business owners that aren't hitting their goals, most of the time it's because their trio is off. They can't work out what the problem is, and end up throwing their attention (not to mention money!) at the wrong problem, when the real issue is right under their nose. If you're thinking any of the below, then you probably have a trio issue:

- "I'm not getting sales, but everything seems fine to me!"
- "I did what other shops in my niche have done, and yet they are making more sales!"
- "I'm getting comments, favourites and good feedback, but no-one is buying!"
- "I launched a new collection, and got crickets *sad face*"
- "Why are people asking me for different variations of what I make?"
- "Why am I getting questions about things, when the answer is right there on the website/listing?"
- "I've been getting some less-than-ideal feedback

recently, what's that about?"
- "I sent my items to an influencer, but I never heard anything back!"

In response to the above, if you are tempted to do any of the following, STOP and read the rest of this chapter first. Do not:

- make some new products
- add some moxie to your graphics
- post a moaning-about-sales post in a Facebook group
- spend money joining a marketing membership
- spend money on someone that claims they can help your listings, but doesn't sell as much as you would like to
- re-do your keywords and SEO (yet again)
- start another social media channel/network
- post your listings on buy-and-sell groups
- do a local village craft fair
- take advice from a fellow seller on something that has worked for them
- "hack" a competitor's Etsy shop by copying their tactics
- shut up shop, and eat chips on the couch

Seriously Boss, the issue is not you. It's not that you're dumb or "can't work this out" (oh hey limiting beliefs!). It's probably just a simple "I haven't encountered this problem yet and need to figure it out" issue.

Coaching Questions:

Looking at these examples, what are your early opinions on what your business may be struggling with (if you have one?)

You may be at the point now where you don't have any of these working for you. In this chapter we are going to be going over each of the three areas of the trio in detail, so don't worry, you'll know the basics by the end of this chapter.

I've added links to some great videos for each of these areas in the Book Bonuses which can be found at www.handmadebosses.com/bookbonus.

TARGET MARKET AND TARGET AUDIENCE

Your target market is essentially the perfect customer who wants to buy what you make; your target audience is who you will market it to. In my experience these end up being roughly the same, so I'll use those terms interchangeably. It's often the first place you should start before you launch your shop, but don't worry, you can reverse-engineer it if you already have a business or store launched.

It's important that you have a good idea as to who your target market is, namely because you then have a clear idea as to what type of products to make, and how to market them correctly so that people vibe with your brand, trust your brand and end up becoming a raving fan. Different people with different backgrounds, personas and preferences react differently to different types of marketing. (Yikes how many times can I say the word differently in one sentence?) But all you need to know is, it takes all sorts to make a world and you need to know what makes your customers tick. Then you know how to reach out to them effectively, and not waste your time, or will create marketing that is "meh" to them. Your perfect target customer will jump for joy, get excited and say "take my money!" when you launch a new product line - this is why it's vital to get this right.

Your target market should go deep into areas like:

- age
- gender
- income group
- job
- marital status
- where they are in the world
- goals
- values
- difficulties or challenges
- pain points

Strictly speaking, the more you dive into target market research, the more things will begin to click for you.

There is a certain amount of generalisation and guesswork when it comes to discovering your target market, which is fine as long as it is educated guesswork. Don't make huge leaps, and if you're in doubt, speak to your target market directly.

Let's use some examples of the power of target market.

EXAMPLE

Janice has a gothic painting shop and loves to paint dark fantasy themed paintings of gremlins, dragons and monsters. She has a very rough idea of her target market (women aged 25-65, that are gothic, and like fantasy paintings) and makes her products based off of that audience. She wonders why she isn't making sales, and one day, is approached by a friend to make a custom order of a lighter, brighter dragon painting. She lists this in her shop and it gets a bit of attention. She then begins to make more of these lighter, airier style of images, but her sales continue to drop. In her mind she made what the people wanted, so why didn't it work?

Simple. Janice didn't have a deep enough understanding of her target market in the first place. The age range was too broad, and so was the description "fantasy paintings". She ended up diluting her target market and attracting the wrong type of person by making products that would actually repel her target market, and she ended up trying to be everything to everyone.

In an alternative universe, Janice instead does this:

She begins with some clues as to who her target market is (women aged 25-65, that are gothic, and like fantasy paintings) and starts to go deeper by looking at her website stats, biggest referrers and Reddit feeds with these different clues. In doing so, she discovers that actually, her target market is:

- a woman aged 30-40
- may have pagan décor in the home
- wears mostly black
- likes incense
- probably has piercings
- likes dragons, gremlins, trolls and witches
- probably doesn't have children, but has cats or reptiles as pets
- her pain point is that conventional paintings and home décor found in the usual shops do not reflect their personality.

When she gets another request to do a lighter brighter painting, she turns it down and instead recommends another artist friend for the job. Instead she buckles down and paints with dragons, gremlins, trolls and witches as the main subject. She also begins to add more black and purple to her brand, and more witch/pagan meme posts to her Instagram profile. She even begins to make some funny comments about paganism and they get reshared hundreds of times. The traffic to her shop increases, and her sales do too, because she has made sure to keep everything consistent with her products and branding.

See how different these two realities can be? All it took was spending more time researching the perfect customer for her products and finding their pain point, and then describing it in one sentence. She effectively went in with the attitude of repelling the wrong people, but attracting the right people.

"If you try to serve everyone, you will serve no-one" is the anthem for this kind of work, and it's better to start super laser-focused on a few people, than starting too broad and being an average store to a lot of people. This might seem counterintuitive because you naturally want to sell a broader variety of products to a bigger segment of people, but actually, the opposite happens. Consider this, it's better to have 500 super-fans who love everything you do and who feel a sense of trust and belonging with your brand (and who will give you a higher conversion rate) than 5000 people that couldn't care less.

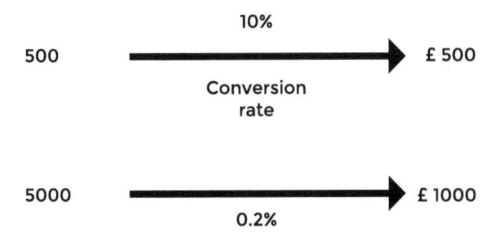

500 →10%→ £ 500

Conversion rate

5000 →0.2%→ £ 1000

Just as a reminder, the conversion rate is the number of people who buy/convert/sign up/do an action you want them to out of how many people view, expressed as a percentage. If 100 people view and one person buys, that's 1%. If 250 people view and three buy, that's 1.2%. Conversion rate can be worked out by dividing the number of purchases/signs ups/conversions by the number of viewers, and then multiply by 100.

Views / Conversions x 100

So, what are some things we need to know about our target market? Try answering some of these questions when doing your research:

Coaching Questions:

1. Are you targeting customers that are male or female?

2. What age are they?

3. Are they single, co-habiting or married?

4. Where do they live?

5. Do they have children?

6. What occupation do they have?

7. What's their average income?

8. What problems do they tend to have?

9. Which of these problems will your product solve?

10. Where do they consume information online?

11. Where do they hang out online?

12. What groups do they belong to?

13. What makes them laugh?

14.   What makes them mad?

A great method of doing this is to research, write down and group certain characteristics together. For example:

- likes dark clothing
- likes dark hair
- has tattoos
- like paganism
- wears pagan cross jewellery
- likes to research tattoos

These could be grouped under these headings:

1.   Likes a dark appearance

2.   Loves tattoo culture

3.   Likes paganism

Coaching Questions:

What are some characteristic groups for your target market?

Once you have done this, it's a good idea to create a target market profile. This is basically compiling all of the information into one A4 size document to quickly consult when you are doing anything that requires you to understand your target market.

Include the information you have found out, and fill in the gaps with the information that you haven't been able to concretely find out (remember, educated guesses are allowed here!) If your research tells you that people like relaxing candles and bubble baths, it's a safe bet that they love taking a bath as a way to relax.

A great way to humanise all of the information that you have found out is to give your ideal target audience a name and a picture. Instead of referencing your target market as "someone who likes baths, relaxing, has two kids, works at an office in Hull etc etc", you can call her Annabelle. Any time you are creating something new, do it for Annabelle. Get enough Annabelles in your store, and you've got yourself a scalable, 6-figure, handmade business, Boss!

Coaching Questions:

Add your own target market profile here:

CHAPTER 8 : THE TERRIFICALLY TANTALISING TRIO

Student Stories

"I decided to start my shop on Etsy in July 2020. I had never run a shop on Etsy before, and in my research and preparation, I came across the Handmade Bosses Success Academy. I was pretty happy already with my brand story and my branding, but I had not really thought about my target market and how important that truly is.

"I found in the competitive landscape section that most of the people buying from similar shops were women, but I was having a hard time figuring out details beyond that. Going through the target market portion of the course gave me good information about what to look for, examples behaviour that could characterize my target market, and ways to figure out more about them. Furthermore, it helped me figure out how to use my target market to my benefit once I understood them better.

"Over time, I learned more details about my target market by studying the customers who were buying my products, how often they were marked as gifts vs bought for themselves, the gift messages that showed various relationships with recipients.

"I have a very clear picture of my target market now: 30-60 year old women who are shopping for a gift - either a non primary relative/friend (niece/nephew/friend's children/etc.) for a significant occasion like a wedding gift, or an immediate family member for a less significant occasion such as anniversaries, Christmas or birthdays, or housewarming gifts.

"Knowing this has helped me tailor my product offerings to the items that this group would buy for someone else, *rather than the items that someone else would buy for this group which was my strategy early on.*

"Without HBSA (Handmade Bosses Success Academy), it would have taken me much, much longer to understand the importance of my target market, and the impact of focusing my offerings on them. Since making the changes, business has exploded, and sales are up 400% year over year for the Christmas rush in November and December. I believe understanding your target market is one of the most important things you can do to help your business."

- Erik Paul, Rocky Mountain Woodcraft

PRODUCTS

You are probably already getting all giddy with the thought of all the things you can make, but before you do, make sure you are creating the right products. This will require a certain amount of testing and guesswork in the beginning, but armed with your target market profile, this should become loads easier. Avoid just running and gunning when making products, there should be a reason they are in your online store (and "because they look cool" doesn't cut it Boss - sorry!)

"But Steph, how do I know what products to make?"

Easy, your products should very strongly relate to your target customer solve a pain point for them, and they should have a unique selling point. Just two ingredients.

Let's jump into pain points first

"Okay, but how do I find out what their pain point is?"

Ah again, easy(ish). A pain point doesn't have to cause your customer physical pain (maybe they should see a doctor rather than a handmade business?) but instead, can cause:

- annoyance
- upset
- sadness
- inconvenience
- anger
- and a lot more!

It's anything that makes them say "ergh" for even a fraction of a second. It's something that your customers themselves may not even be aware of. If they don't, it's your job to shine a light on that pain point and introduce your product as the solution.

There are different types of pain points I've identified in the industry, the top three being:

- Pain point relating to process - how something is done, how easy it is, how quickly it's done etc.
- Financial pain point - something that is costing them more than they'd like
- Emotional pain point - something that's causing them emotional pain, like being sad, angry or missing something.
- Let's play a game of spot the pain point to make sure we've got this:

- Janet's car is always smelly and she hates getting in it in the morning
- Henry hates the fact that his chopping board looks so ugly
- Fredrica would love it if her makeup was all in one place
- Wendy misses the forests of her hometown, now she lives in the big city with no green space
- Isabelle thinks that the paper industry could do more to help save trees.

Answer - all of them!

All of them are pain points and all of those people would be attracted to a product that solves their pain point.

Remember though, people's purchasing habits are driven by emotion, so it's a good idea to make it as emotion-driven as possible.

Coaching Questions:

What are some pain points that people in your target market have?

What pain points does your product solve?

NOW, LET'S CONSIDER YOUR USP (UNIQUE SELLING POINT)

A unique selling point is something that makes you different from your competitor. It's what sways (or will sway) your customer towards you, rather than the competitor. It could be something as small as the process you use to create something (for example, soy wax candles) or something related to how you use something (using a bookmark as a letter opener) or even the way you position a product (promoting crystal necklaces for business health). Whatever your USP, you have to make sure to put that at the forefront of your products and marketing.

Something that many bosses struggle with is the notion of having to create something new and reinvent the wheel. You don't. In fact, I wouldn't recommend creating something new, if it's not proven to be something consumers want. All you have to do is find an existing aspect of your business or product that makes your business stand out - even in a crowded market. I have a fair bit of experience in this, my Etsy shop was the first to create a specific type of jewellery product, and within two years, I had inadvertently started a jewellery trend on the platform in an extremely saturated niche.

To find your unique selling point, you have to look at what you do well as a business, and what your customers want. It's also a great idea to look at your competitors too, to see what they don't do, that you do.

To start, note down in detail your creation process from A-Z. Then look at your target customer and what they want. Finally, write what you do well (or what others say you do well!) You will start to see some crossovers and clues as to the reason why people do and will flock to you.

LET'S LOOK AT AN EXAMPLE

Patricia has a planner shop where she has created journals and planners for business owners. She has noticed that reviews seem to mention that she arranges things in the planners in a very orderly and clear way, which makes planning easy for her customers. She knows that her customers are busy mum-preneurs who need to get organised quickly, or it'll never happen.

After looking at her competitors, she sees that they over-complicate planning, and make it all about reflection exercises, rather than just getting on with planning. After a short while, she emails a few of her previous customers (as well as friends and family) and confirms her suspicion that she thinks differently, and because of that, her planning process is unique to her. This is her USP.

However Patricia, don't go thinking "That's it, we just need to present it in a better way than that." Word your USP in an attractive promise, such as "To-the-point planning for productivity not procrastination" or "Plan your year in 24 hours or less".

Wording your USP in an attractive way makes it catchy and easy to remember; it ensures that your target market remembers your business, and you become the go-to for your product. Let's look at some more examples:

- "Candles that are better for your health than normal wax candles" instead becomes "Healthy candles".
- "Jewellery that will make you remember your childhood trips to the woods" becomes "Bring a childhood memory with you always".
- "Hair bands to tie your hair up in style" becomes "Say 'bye to bad hair days in 10 seconds or less".

See how these are the same "promises" - just worded differently? If you need a little help with this, try leading with the promise, followed by the time frame or the way your product will deliver the promise.

Coaching Questions:

What's your creation process?

What's different from how others do it?

What's your USP?

What's your promise?

BRANDING

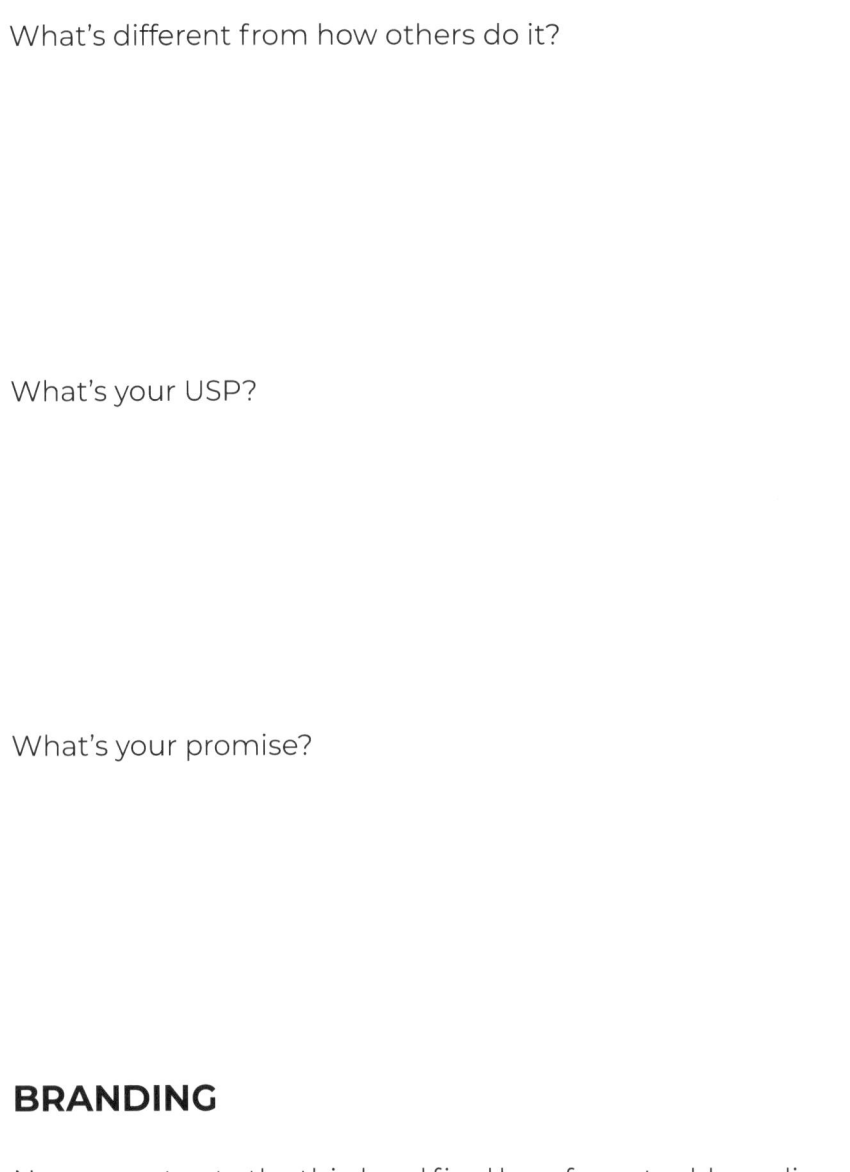

Now we get onto the third and final leg of our stool, branding. Branding is what ties everything together into one neat little package. Not only that, but it attracts your target market to your shop with ease. People do tend to over-complicate branding, but it's so much more than just your logo.

In summary, your brand should have:

- a logo that makes sense to your target audience, and makes it obvious what you make and what your business is called
- brand colours (no more than 4) that make everything consistent across your business
- fonts that again, make everything consistent
- a tagline that gets your message across and that may also contain a call for your target market, or advertises your USP
- a message that communicates a set of values to your customer; this is the thing that convinces your customers that they belong with your brand, and that you made your products specifically for them
- product images that show off your crafts, while also still being on-brand and attractive.

This all may sound super-overwhelming for sure, but really, your brand has one super-simple aim: to attract your target audience to you, and communicate that you have the same values they have, and that you have something they need in their lives, namely, your product.

Branding has multiple touchpoints:

- banners
- website
- business cards
- packaging
- social media
- labels
- emails etc…

… so it's important to make sure that your branding is

consistent across all of the places where your customer is likely to come in contact with your brand. This avoids the feeling of confusion (the ultimate turn-off for paying customers) and ensures that you build that ultimate trust factor.

Let's go over each of the brand elements, and ways you can make sure you create it in the best way.

BRAND MESSAGE

This is the core message that your brand stands for (not to be confused with tagline) and is something that ideally should match up with what your target market stands for too. This is the overall feel that you want to get across and is actually super-subtle. For example, Coca Cola's brand message is "better together", and this is reflected in their ad campaigns and branding where they are showing people getting together over an ice cold Coke. Red Bull's is "this drink gives you enough energy to feel like you're flying", again, reinforced by their ads and funny slogans. Your brand message has to convey something that you will always stand for in your business. Whilst colours, fonts and images can be changed, your brand message really should be a permanent fixture of your business.

Coaching Questions:

Try answering these questions to find your brand message:

- What do I stand for that my target market does too?

- What kind of people do I want to attract?

- What kind of mindset will they have?

- What's my USP?

- What does my brand and product promise?

- If someone was to describe my brand in two years' time, what words would I like them to use?

- What is the mission for my business?

- If someone gave me 30 seconds to describe my business, what would I say?

Make sure before you go ahead and create the other branding elements, that you have an idea of your brand message

TAGLINE

This is a sentence that will sit under your full logo and be the core message of your company. The power of this is huge, especially when you stick to it and use it as the brand "north star".

Coaching Questions:

Begin by answering the following questions:

- What do I sell?

- Who is it for?

- What does my business promise?

- What is my customer pain point that I solve with this promise?

From there, start to craft a short tagline that gets across everything you need to convey in a short, snappy sentence. For example, let's look at how we would craft a tagline for a t-shirt business that makes matching tees for mothers and their daughters:

- What do I sell? Matching t-shirts for mothers and daughters
- Who is it for? Mothers of a daughter
- What does my business promise? To savour and deepen the bond between a mother and her mini-me
- What is my customer pain point that I solve with this promise? That time is flying by and the little girl is growing up fast; the mother wants to capture a moment in time, and display her daughter proudly as her mini-me

Tagline: "Proudly presenting my mini-me".

See how we simply took words and phrases that stood out to create a shortened version? Now we have done the background/behind the scenes work, it's time to move on to the design aspects of branding.

Coaching Questions:

What's my tagline?

COLOURS

Your brand colours are a vehicle for your brand's feeling; if chosen incorrectly, they could really mess up the vibe you're trying to go for with your business. When it comes to brand colours, every colour has a meaning in your customer's head. For example, when we see red and yellow, we think of McDonald's, right? What about purple and white? Cadburys. What if we switched those two brand colours over? It would seem almost... wrong somehow.

This is why it's important to have a base knowledge of colour theory, and how different colours give us different feelings:

- red - passion, bold, excitement, anger, importance and attention
- orange - playful, friendly, warmth and vitality
- yellow - cheerful, sunshine, summer, positivity, joyful
- green - balance, healthy, natural, eco, fresh, growth
- blue - trustworthy, secure, sturdy, peaceful, smart
- purple - royal, wise, nostalgic, hippy, gothic
- black - prestige, serious, classic, simple, sassy, mysterious

Don't get me wrong, there are some outliers that sit outside of these colours, but to get you started, those are some feelings that I get when I look at logos with these colours.

When choosing your brand colours, it helps to choose based on these criteria:

- Base colours (1 or 2) - these colours are your go-to colours that people will eventually come to think of "your" colours. Whenever they see this colour, they will

think of you. Also, they are used as the main ingredient for design elements on websites, social media and in your logo
- Accent colour (1 or 2) - colour(s) that you also include with your base colours; they can be used to highlight important information, and draw people's eyes to an important design element
- Neutral (1) - great for things like website backgrounds and areas that have to be pretty simple; don't overthink this one - if in doubt, choose white.

Next, create your brand palette. My favourite three tools for this are Pinterest, a copy of the colour wheel, and Coolors (coolors.co). I'll first begin by searching what I sell, or a vibe I'm going for, and start to make notes and save pins of colours I like (kind of like a brand moodboard). Then I'll head to Coolors and begin to find complementary colours, monochromatic colours, analogous colours or triadic colours to sit alongside them.

- Monochromatic - one colour in many different shades. Great if you've found one brand colour you want to heavily roll with
- Triadic and complementary - two or three colours that sit roughly opposite each other in a colour wheel
- Analogous - colours that nicely sit next to each other in class - I mean, the colour wheel.

This may take some time and you can have a play around, but eventually you will have a palette of 3-4 brand colours that you love, and that gets #allthefeels across to your customer. Once you have, don't forget to save the hex code somewhere (should look something like this #0005HY)!

Coaching Questions:

What's my brand base colour?

Accent colour?

Neutrals?

What are the hex codes for the exact shades I'm going for?

FONTS

Now, I'm no font expert, and I know for a fact that you don't need to know all the fancy types of fonts out there, so in the interests of keeping it simple, choose two fonts for two different purposes:

- Main font - used for your logo and/or tagline. This is the star of the show when it comes to your brand's typeface. Must be easy to read.
- Accent font - a bit fancier, and used for accent information, or complementary information. Must be able to be read, and a contrast from the first font.

The easiest way to do this is to get stuck in and test out a load of fonts. Write your business name and tagline in editing software such as Canva or Photoshop, and start changing the fonts until you get a few combos you like.

Hint: I tend to have one "sans serif" font, and one "handwriting" style font.

If you get stuck, check out your competitors and other brands you admire, and make sure that the final fonts you choose can be read on small and large screens correctly - there's nothing worse than a logo no-one can see when it's small!

Coaching Questions:

What's my brand's main font?

What's my brand's accent font?

LOGO

This will likely be one of the first touchpoints that your customer sees when they first interact with you. This has to convey 3-4 things using the colours and fonts you have chosen:

- your brand overall message/vibe
- your tagline
- your business name
- what you sell

This sounds like a tall order, but there are some sneaky ways this can be done. There's no easy way to start, other than just heading to a design programme or website such as Canva or (or using good ol' fashioned pencil and paper) and just start drawing. Begin with reminding yourself where your logo will be used, your chosen fonts and colours, and start playing around typing your business name and tagline in different combos.

Some things to remember:

- Create an all-white and all-black version of your logo, just in case you ever need it for different uses.
- Download the logo without a background (PNG file) as well as a JPG.
- Ask yourself if the logo will look good on your likely packaging (more on this later).
- If in doubt, go simple. Do a simple logo with some pictorial elements or Clipart all in one colour.
- If it looks too wordy, get rid of the tagline.
- If it looks too simple, try creating an emblem (something that gets the message across without using words).
- Is it obvious what it is with just a glance? People may only look at your logo for one second, so it's got be glaringly obvious and simple. Test it by scrolling past it and see if it catches your eye.
- Is it different from your competitors? Will people get you confused with them if it's too similar?
- Avoid the cliché generic-type logos. Just because you crochet, it doesn't mean your logo has to have a ball of yarn in it.
- If you get super stuck, try hiring a graphic designer to create one for you (there are some fab ones on Etsy).

Coaching Questions:

Sketch your logo here:

PRODUCT IMAGES (PHOTOGRAPHY)

No pressure, but your product images are the only "contact" your target audience will have with your product before they purchase. Eeeeek! However, now you've completed all of the other previous brand elements, this should be a breeze. The best place to start is to develop your signature photography style; this is something especially important if you are selling on a marketplace or somewhere similar, as you will potentially be pitted against many other handmade businesses all competing for attention. So developing a signature style will train customers' eyes to spot your product amongst others.

Let me be clear, you do not need an expensive digital camera to take decent images. Recently, I challenged my friend to do a product photoshoot of her Etsy shop products with just her iPhone and light editing – her shots turned out as good as my DSLR images! In fact, I placed them side by side and we couldn't tell the difference. Phones are getting better on-board camera equipment every year, which really helps with this whole process.

So, what do you need to take great images?

- A tripod - no matter how slow you think you can breathe, you cannot prevent movement as well as a tripod can.
- A light source - natural is best, but avoid direct sunlight that will create shadows. If in doubt, go near a window on a bright, but cloudy day. This will diffuse the sunlight. If you live somewhere dark, or you don't have anywhere suitable, you can pick up a pair of inexpensive daylight

photography lights online; in fact, the two I use to shoot my YouTube videos were £40 for two!
- A camera or phone camera
- Background - I always recommend to keep it simple - a maximum of two things in shot behind the product at a time (for example a textured background and one prop); too much can be distracting otherwise. A white background is nice, but for handmade products, having some brand personality always converts best.
- Props that make sense - have a collection of props that make sense for your images. Bath bomb images make sense next to water, a bookmark makes sense next to a book and homemade teas make sense next to a mug. Try to find props that are in your brand colours.

Ok Boss, so now that you know what you need, it's time to play around with imagery.

1. Before you begin, gather up all of the things that you need to take images of. I recommend batching product images to save time. Also create a shot list if you want to take multiple images of each item (I've detailed one below).

2. Start by taking some sample images with different light settings (exposure, contrast and brightness etc.) Keep going and comparing until you find lighting styles that work the best.

3. Then start to play around with the amount and position of props until you get a style that you like - compare these with each other.

4. Once you have a style picked, grab your target market and brand profiles and make sure that they all complement and make sense to each other.

5. Begin taking pictures!

You may not get perfect imagery right on the first try, but after practising, you'll be sure to nail the perfect product images.

There is so much more when it comes to product photography, and different images styles you can utilise for different purposes in your business. Here's a ready-made shot list for you below:

- Product shots - pretty simple: simply take images of the product from different angles.
- Lifestyle shots - more props added, demonstrate what this product would look like "in the wild".
- Option shots - showing the different options or variations if applicable.
- Detail shots - showing any notable detail of the item.
- Modelled shots - enlist the help of a professional model or friend, and get them to model your item for you - this shows relative size and enables customers to visually see how the product would look.

Coaching Questions:

What do I need to source for my photography?

What type of images will I be taking?

What feeling do I need these images to invoke?

Chapter 9

PERFECT PACKAGING

Now you have an idea as to where you will sell, and you know all about the "winning trio", it's time to begin thinking about how you will package your item. Packaging is super important because it's the first contact your customer will have with your brand, and the unboxing experience has to be epic. Think about the last time you received something in a bubble mailer with no personality. Remember what vendor you bought it from? Nope, didn't think so. What about the last time you received something that was presented in a way that made you gasp and say "Oooh, that's fancy!"? You remember straight away where it was from.

Handmade bosses are usually in one of two camps when it comes to packaging:

1. "I'm going to spend weeks researching perfect branded and coloured tissue, get custom-printed boxes and make sure the box sings Beyonce when they open it." (Ok, the last bit was exaggerated).

Or

2. "I'll just whack it in a bubble mailer bag, job done".

Space for your notes

Both of these aren't ideal, mainly because you're either spending too much time and money on something and obsessing over it, or because you don't care about the first interaction your customer will have with your company.

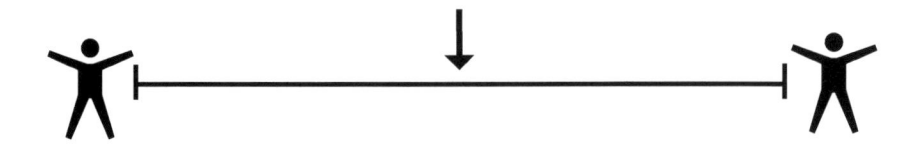

Packaging doesn't have to cost the earth, nor does it have to be super boring; with a few simple tricks, you can create packaging perfection. There are two jobs with packaging, the first is to protect the item when it's going through the postal network, the second is to carry on your brand vibe and message right through until the customer opens it. This seems challenging for sure, but in all honesty, it's not that difficult once you get in the groove.

The truth is, we can create gorgeous packaging with just a little bit of time and creativity (which luckily, as creatives we have lots of!)

Coaching Questions:

So, let's begin to create our packaging by first answering these questions:

1. What do I need to protect when my item is being delivered through the post? (cardboard, bubble wrap, tissue etc.)

2. What areas are likely to get damaged if I don't package properly? (corners, glass, tangled jewellery etc.)

3. What kind of feeling do I want my packaging to give? (relate this back to your brand feeling.)

4. What kind of textures, colours and material would I need to use to get that feeling? (shiny, card, eco-friendly, pink, purple, material etc.)

5. What do I want my packaging to include? (business cards, leaflets, samples, ribbon, gift tags etc.)

6. If I were to offer an upgraded packaging option for a fee, what would this have in addition to the normal packaging option? (ribbon, upgraded box etc.)

Now you have an idea of what your packaging has to have, begin to sketch out some ideas, or head to Pinterest and search "X packaging ideas". I have even made a Pinterest collage board of simple packaging ideas for you, this can be found in the Book Bonuses: (www.handmadebosses.com/bookbonus)

From checking out examples, you can start to gain more of an idea and jump-off points for your packaging.

Make sure to begin with what your packaging needs to include; if there are any delicate areas, start with figuring out how to protect those, then build your brand vibe, colours etc. into your packaging afterwards.

If you are tempted to get custom boxes printed - stop. These can range from £3-£8 each depending on quantity ordered and size. Unless you are starting a very high-end business, I would recommend starting with the basics first. A box doesn't have to be logo-printed, perhaps a sticker or rubber stamp could achieve the same effect? Or get custom-branded tissue, which would be tons cheaper than boxes. Or if your brand vibe allows it, embrace the minimalist vibe.

You don't even have to have your logo on it at all - why not add some oomph with twine, ribbon, stickers, tissue, shredded tissue or gift tags? All of these can be found for less than 10p each use, and still give the same "wow" effect.

After working with a wide range of handmade business owners, I've helped many people with their packaging, so I've compiled a list of common packages, along with some ideas we had for adding flair to them:

- Prints - plain cardboard box with plastic sleeve, sticker,

shredded tissue, business card.
- Jewellery - bubble mailer bag with stamped box, ribbon, gift tag and business card.
- T-shirts - large bubble mailer bag or mailer with tissue around the shirt, sticker to fix it, and a business card.
- Face cream - medium-size box with shredded tissue, instructions for use and a small sample.
- Bath bomb - small box with shockproof cardboard packaging, shredded tissue and business card.

Below, I've also added some common packaging elements with the rough prices I would be expecting to pay. These can vary by location, quantity, customisation degree and date, but should give you a rough idea:

- business cards - 5p each
- business leaflet - 10p each
- small cardboard boxes - 30p each
- medium boxes - 60p each
- large boxes - £1+
- shredded tissue - £2 for 50g
- plain tissue paper - 5p per sheet
- logo-printed tissue - 80p per sheet
- DVD-size bubble mailer bags - 20p each
- plain gift tags - 6p each
- rubber stamp and ink (one-time purchase) £30

You can see how packaging really doesn't have to be expensive to be effective. Just making sure that it fits with your brand message can be a super simple way to deliver your products to your customers safely.

Be sure to order some samples and do a test-run of your packaging. I like to do a dummy order with complete packaging and mail it to myself. That way, I know exactly how it would arrive to the customer. You can also drop it from standing height ten times and open it to see if the product has been damaged; if so, add some more protection as, after all, the packaging's primary aim is to protect the product in transit.

Coaching Questions:

What things will I need to include in my packaging?

How much will these things individually cost (break them down).

Sketch some packaging ideas below:

"Steph, what do I put on business cards/leaflets?"

This is a question I get asked regularly, and honestly, it really depends on a few factors. But here's a list of some ideas on what to put on business cards/leaflets:

- A discount code for their next purchase. Studies have shown that customers that have bought from you before are a great deal more likely to place another order soon afterward.
- Your web address. Start to build traffic for your web address when you purchase a domain, or use a built-in address for your marketplace store. If you have chosen to sell on Etsy, you can link a custom domain to your Etsy shop.
- An email address. In case they have any questions or queries.
- A design that fits in with your branding. Use the same fonts, colours and imagery that are reflected in your brand. Include your logo.
- Your social media channel(s). Where can they continue the relationship and learn more about your business? Don't forget to include a blog if you have one.
- Care information or instructions. If your product requires some extra love and attention or more information to use it, make sure to include that.

Coaching Questions:

What will you put on your business packaging inserts/business card?

Chapter 10

PAINLESS PRICING

You may start to create your products, or have an idea of what you would like to create, but the next question is, how can I price profitably? Despite some popular coaches telling you that pricing formulas work, they actually don't. Why? Well mainly because they only look at the monetary number you spend on the item, multiply that by a certain amount, check what others are doing and leave it at that. But the problem here is that this sets you up to fail, mainly because you are totally governed by what others are doing in the marketplace, and you end up with a low profit margin. Instead, us handmade bosses have done the work to create a gorgeous product to solve a pain point for the customer, now let's charge what it's worth.

"Perceived value pricing" is something that many successful brands undertake, and it ensures that your project remains profitable. Really think about it: if Tiffany charged just twice what their raw materials cost for creating their products, then the price tags would be a fraction of what they are today. However, you would value the product less, it would be less coveted.

The same with Rolex. The raw materials are pretty cheap (compared to the markup) yet value is added by increasing the price.

Space for your notes

Apple computers, the same deal. It costs the same to build a basic cheap PC as a basic powerful PC (with raw materials) but it's the brand and extras that Apple add that gives it its fancy flair.

But let me ask you this, what would happen if all of these companies slashed their prices overnight? People would say:

- "What's wrong with it for it to be that cheap?"
- "It's obviously not as good as the more expensive option."
- "It must be bad quality."
- "It'll more than likely break."

This is in fact what handmade business owners do when they charge a low price for what they offer. They think they will get more sales through the door, but the reality is that they will get less, as the product will be perceived as lesser quality. Not only this, but many bosses have reported that when they dropped their prices, they received more complaints, worse reviews and more follow-up questions. To top it off, you're not going to be making enough of a profit to reinvest back into your business, which is the lifeblood of business growth. To sum up in a sentence: Your pricing tells people how seriously you take your work, and how seriously you want your work to be taken.

Let's look at a real-life example:

Jennifer creates organic aromatherapy hand creams for people with anxiety and dry skin. She has trained in aromatherapy and is a beauty therapist. When she looked at her baseline costs, they were:

- materials: 40p per unit
- time: £1.30 per unit
- fees: 50p per unit
- shipping: £1 per unit
- packaging 60p per unit

That totals £3.80 per unit.

If she were to just double it, she would be charging £7.60, with £3.80 profit per unit sold. Certainly not enough to create any decent growth.

What about tripling it? That would be £11.40 with £7.60 profit per unit. Not bad, but could be better.

Instead, Jennifer looks at the pain point she solves, her brand and expertise. She realises that through her target market research, 50% of people that have dry skin, suffer with anxiety, so she creates a product specifically for those people to do a "two-in-one" job. She believes that aromatherapy can help many people with anxiety, and has created her own blend of lavender, peppermint and rose to help calm the nerves and level the mind. She asks in a few Facebook anxiety groups and gets to know a few people in there, as well as being a sufferer herself. She hears stories of cancelled job interviews, horrible flights and flunked exams, all because of anxiety. She realises that this is a huge pain point for her target market (one that could potentially affect their lives deeply) and ponders this important question: "What would someone pay to solve this pain point?" Well, a lot more than £11.40 for sure.

She decides to price her product at £19.95 for the small size, and £26.95 for the larger size, and positions it as an aromatherapy two-in-one product. That means for every unit sold, she gets from £16.15 to £23.15 profit.

Furthermore, if she creates five orders a day, that's:

£80.75 - 115.75 profit a day

£565.25 - £810.25 profit a week

£29,393 - £42,133 profit a year

cue excited happy dance

"But Steph, my customer won't pay that much!"

Here's the thing Boss, if you get messages or comments from people saying, "I wouldn't pay that much for that," great. That means that your trio (see the trio chapter in this book) is working well enough to repel the wrong people and attract the right people.

Listen, I'm not saying that it's going to come super easily, but you have to know your worth. Yes, your customers could go to Tesco or Walmart and get hand cream for £1. Cool. They are not your target market. Your target market is those people that have a deep need for your product, a person who connects with your brand values and a person that you communicate your worth to effectively.

In fact, here's an exercise for you to do. Every time someone comments something like:

- "Ooft! That's a lot of money!"
- "I could make that for half the price!"
- "I would never pay that"

... simply say aloud or in your head, "Great! That means my trio is working well!"

HOW TO ACTUALLY PRICE YOUR PRODUCTS

OK, so this all sounds great, but how should we actually price our products? Well, rather than a formula, I've put together a strategy:

BASELINE COSTS

- Your time. How long it takes you to make a product - this has monetary value too! I would recommend paying yourself an hourly wage as a guideline.
- Your material costs. What is actually used to make the product a reality.
- Your fees. Your Etsy fees and any other fees you have.
- Your shipping / postage costs etc.
- Your packaging - boxes, add-ons etc.

MARKET VALUE

The highest and lowest price that people are willing to pay. Look at your competition.

How strong is your brand? Consider your branding here, as your brand adds value.

How BIG your customer's pain point is. This affects things

massively here. For example, let's say we make hair bows for little girls for weddings. The pain point is that the bride wants an easy way to make the little flower girl's hair pretty, yet can be adjusted throughout the day as they run around, play and get their hair messed up. She also wants a keepsake for her flower girls. You can see how this is a stronger pain point than just "an everyday hair bow".

You want to aim for the top end of the market value. So, say you see people are charging between £10-£100 for something, then aim for the £80-£100 mark.

DISCOUNT WIGGLE ROOM

This is the small monetary or percentage wiggle room that you put on your products. This could be used for the occasional shipping overage, a discount, or a sale.

Now it's your turn, create a list or spreadsheet that you'll use whenever you're considering creating a new product, even before you have purchased the materials.

Baseline	Costs	Market	Value	Discount	Wiggle Room
Time	£	Low	£		
Materials	£	High	£		
Fees	£	Average	£		
Shipping	£	Mine	£		
Packaging	£		£		

If you have looked at your pricing and realised that you need to reduce some costs, that's fine. Make sure you are not compromising your brand's message and values as you are cutting costs however. Some common places where Bosses need to cut costs are:

1. materials

2. packaging

3. shipping

Let's go into some ways you can cut costs for each of these below:

MATERIALS

Otherwise known as the bare essentials that you require to make the product. Sometimes when we first start, we will go to local hobby and craft shops to purchase what we need. However, what we don't know is that there is already a pretty hefty markup on these materials. Instead, I would recommend purchasing from wholesale sources in bulk. There are two places I tend to look to find wholesale suppliers:

- Wholesale shows and exhibitions stockists' lists. Look online for local wholesale shows (find a list of my favourites in the makers' toolkit that can be found in the Book Bonuses) and then navigate to the stockists' lists. There you will find a list of people that exhibit at the shows and their websites/contact information.

- Online searches. Google "X wholesalers" or "X bulk buy" to start to get clues as to where you can find what you need.

PACKAGING

As mentioned in the packaging chapter, this is a great and simple way to cut costs. Again, try and purchase what you need in bulk to drive down per unit costs, and check places like Amazon, Etsy and Ebay for cheaper supplies and bulk buys.

SHIPPING

Is there an alternative carrier you could use? A way to cut costs by using a different service? Or a way to package your item so it fits in a smaller shipping category?

Coaching Questions:

Add your own packaging costs here:

Student Stories

"When I first started my business in 2016, I had no idea how much I should charge for my prints. So, I went to Etsy and looked at other print shops and charged slightly under what they charged. I thought this was the best way to price my prints, but it turned out that this was one of many mistakes that I made in my business. I thought that I had to beat my competitors by charging less than them, but I was so wrong.

"I wondered why I wasn't getting many sales, and I certainly wasn't making any profit on the sales that I did make. At this point I was desperate and needed help to turn my expensive hobby into a business.

"I found Handmade Bosses on YouTube and enrolled in the course. The pricing module was invaluable to me. Not only did I learn to price my items correctly, but I was actually making a profit and was able to start investing in high-quality equipment. My business took off then, and shortly after, I was able to leave my NHS job and take my print business full time.

"Handmade Bosses allowed me to fulfil my dream of running my own business, and I will be forever grateful to Steph for this."

- **Sophie, The English Print Co.**

WHAT ARE YOUR *thoughts?*

Chapter 11

SUPERB STORYTELLING

Picture this: you are walking along the street when you realise you have nothing for dinner. You are walking past a local bakery when you remember your promise to yourself: to eat a balanced diet. Damn, the cronuts will have to wait another day. You then spot a local greengrocer's up the road and hurry past the tempting doughnut shop toward the smell of green before sugar tempts you back into its clutches.

You enter the greengrocers to find paper bags, fresh veggies, and behind the counter, the classic shopkeeper wearing an apron. She smiles at you and says "Good afternoon, welcome! Everything is organic here, and grown by me. My name is Sheila, let me know if you want any help!"

Wow, you think, this is so nice! After wandering around for a couple of minutes, you notice some heavenly-looking corn on the cob, a bit pricy at £2 a cob, but when it looks this good, you almost don't care. You ask Sheila how to cook it without it being as hard as a house brick; she happily comes over and lets you know how best to cook the corn on the cob for optimum taste and texture. She even writes the instructions down on a piece of paper.

You then proceed to pick out a veggie side dish and take it to the till. While she's carefully packaging up your dinner, she tells you that her grandfather owned a farm in the Cotswolds that she used to help with as a little girl. She has had plants passed down from generations, and secret pest-repellent techniques using organic means. She tells you what will be in season next month and offers some simple home recipes for you to try when you come back to purchase the Braeburn apples she will be hosting next month. You pay Sheila, thank her and pick up her business card.

That was 100% worth paying the extra, and the car journey.

Now picture this: you head to your local superstore, where you are met with an aura of industrial white and grey. You grab a trolley, with a busted wheel of course, and head to the aisles with your list. You endlessly parade up and down searching for what you need, when you ask a member of staff for help. They tell you it's on aisle 35. You finish up your shopping and head to the checkout.

A beyond-bored checkout assistant throws your shopping at lightning speed down the packer, and before you even finish packaging your shopping, says in a monotone voice, "That's £15.87." You fumble for your credit card, as people glare at you from the queue for taking too long, and eventually tap your card to pay. The checkout assistant throws you the receipt and proceeds with the next person. On the way out you realise you need milk, but as you look back into the massive shop, you can't bear to face another supermarket-sweep style food shop. "Forget the milk," you say, and go home to consume the bruised and tasteless veggies you have just purchased.

Ok, so it's pretty obvious which one you are more likely to go to again, and the point of these stories is to outline how important owning your story is. So many business owners try to make themselves look like a bigger company than they are, but in all honesty, it's all about the quality of business you own, not the quality of your employees or stock. All of this can be translated to your customer through your business story, and this is what we will be discussing in this chapter.

Your story is the cornerstone of your business, and actually is what sets you apart from the big box stores. Think about the difference between your favourite local shop and the big box stores. Is it the human connection? Expert advice? High-quality goods? It's probably a mixture of all three. People care about your story, and if they don't, they aren't in your target market. Period.

Your story has the power to:

- build trust
- connect with your target market on a level that big box stores can't
- position yourself as the expert
- introduce yourself effectively
- educate people who have never heard of you, why you are so great at what you do.

Some common mistakes that I see when people write their story is that they either make it too short, or too long. Honestly, there's no golden number, but around 400-600 words is ideal. You want to keep your story on point, but also don't skimp on details that will connect with your customer on an emotional level (remember, most purchases are emotional, not logical!)

Let's look at some examples of a "bad" expression of a business story, vs a good one:

> Shop: Laura's Leggings
>
> Sells on: Etsy
>
> Open since 2020

"Hi, I'm Laura. I started making leggings during the lockdown of 2020, and I loved it so much I decided to make a hobby out of it. Please note all orders are dispatched within two working days

Thanks for shopping!"

VS:

"Laura's Leggings: stand-out leggings for all shapes and sizes!

"The story of Laura's Leggings began back in 2016 when I was struggling immensely to find a pair of non-boring leggings. Every shop I went in sold one type: the classic black legging. Whilst these were lovely and practical, I wanted something a bit different. You see, I'm a blue-haired "out of the box" kind of lass, and I wanted my clothing to reflect that – life's too short for boring leggings!

"In 2020 during the lockdown after my last pair of leggings ripped, I decided enough was enough! I borrowed my mum's sewing machine, and tirelessly worked to create the pattern for what is now our classic Laura Legging; stretchy, comfy and lovingly loud. After testing these leggings for months, I finally found the perfect stitching,

fabric and thread to make these leggings super durable - it's like I had found the magic formula!

"I happily recycled my old boring leggings, and began sporting my own leggings wherever I went - go me! After getting stopped by five women on my way to the supermarket to ask where I had got mine from, within hours I realised - I needed to make these for other women too! That's where Laura's Leggings was born!

"My vision is to reinvent boring leggings and bring some pizazz to any outfit without skimping on comfort, and that's exactly what we do with our patented legging creation process.

"Follow me on Insta @LoveLaurasLeggings for behind the scenes and outfit advice for lazy dressers like me!"

I hope by now you can easily see the difference between the two stories and the emotional punch they pack!

Just a note: don't include any logistical information in your story, such as shipping info and other shopping information; this will disconnect the customer from your story and suddenly make it seem like a commodity rather than a pleasure-read.

So now let's get to work creating your own story for your business with these "building blocks".

An ideal story should:

1. include your business name and mission statement (a short sentence or two describing your aim for your business)

2. detail the back story of you as a person

3. detail the back story of the business

4. highlight the pain point you had

5. connect with the customer's pain point

6. talk about what you do now, and the vision for the company

7. talk about why people should buy from you over other businesses using your USP

8. tell them where they can follow up with you

These will act as the main paragraphs for your story. In the space below, write your story building blocks to begin crafting your brand story.

Coaching Questions:

Use this list to craft your brand's story building blocks:

- What is your business name and mission statement (a short sentence or two describing your aim for your business)

- Detail the back story of you as a person

- Detail the back story of the business

- Highlight the pain point you had

- Connect with the customer's pain point

- Talk about what you do now, and the vision for the company

- Talk about why people should buy from you over other businesses, using your USP

- Tell them where they can follow up with you

What's your final brand story?

WHAT ARE YOUR *thoughts?*

Chapter 12

KICK-BUTT KEYWORDS & SEARCH

There will be two moods when reading this chapter, dread or excitement. You'll either be itching to get the secrets that will bring floods of eyeballs to your shop, or you will have anxiety just looking at the word SEO (search engine optimisation). But bosses, SEO is really not that hard, and it isn't the be-all-and-end-all either. Put simply, it's just another way to drive traffic and market your shop through ranking highly on search engines (places like Google, YouTube, Etsy etc.)

SEO can be called many things so don't be alarmed if you hear it named slightly differently:

- search engine optimisation
- keyword research
- search terms
- index hacking
- increasing ranking
- query matching

Again, let me say this a different way: search engine optimisation is just another way of improving aspects of your web presence so that more people can find you. That's it. It's like popping a flag on your head in a busy airport to help people find you easier.

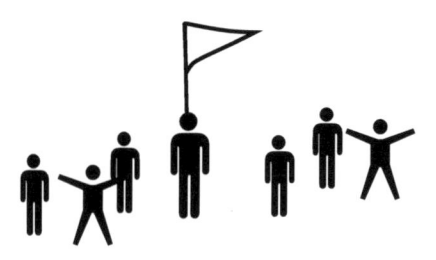

Before we begin, let's bust some scary-looking SEO jargon.

ORGANIC AND PAID TRAFFIC

You may also hear terms like "organic" and "paid traffic"; that's a little outside of the scope of this book, and something you shouldn't really worry about until you're ready to scale, but organic traffic is just another word for "free traffic", it's traffic that you get through free means such as social media or content. Paid traffic is traffic you pay for with things like ads or sponsorship. SEO is commonly used to get more organic traffic to your business, and you're utilising what people are already searching for, on common places they search for it, and position yourself within the results. If the search matches what the person is actually looking for (this can be different depending on what language they use) then they will get results for their query.

KEYWORDS AND SEARCH TERMS

You've probably heard words like "keywords" and "search terms"; these are just ways to describe what words you should use (or how a customer would) to describe your item.

Some keywords are "good" whereas some are "bad".

EXAMPLE:

If you are searching for a gold heart necklace:

Bad: "heart necklace"

Vague, does not accurately describe what it is the customer is searching for, may encourage the customer to leave the search and look elsewhere.

Good: "Gold polished heart locket necklace"

Precise, long-tail, customer is later in their search and knows exactly what they want and is more likely to buy.

KEYWORD STUFFING

Nothing to do with cooking a roast, but equally just as bad if you get it all wrong. Keyword stuffing is a massive no-no in the SEO world. Basically, it's where you go all-out SEO mad, and put ALL the keywords in one short space. Search engines recognise this and can blacklist your website.

EXAMPLE:

Gold necklace silver necklace heart necklace shiny gold chain for woman heart pendant for her

LONG-TAIL KEYWORDS AND SHORT-TAIL KEYWORDS

Said to be named after the tail of a dinosaur, long-tail keywords are those that are present later in the search of something. So they commonly have more descriptive words (or more words in general) and they are usually the kind of searches you do when you know pretty well exactly what you want.

EXAMPLES:

Short-tail - "scarf" - very broad, won't get many purchasing customers with this one.

Long-tail - "Silk pink heart large scarf" - customer knows what they want, will probably buy/click something that pops up for this search.

KEYWORD RESEARCH

This is how you find those perfect keywords to use within your website. Research IS needed, but the good news is that it's easier than you think (more on this later).

CRAWLED OR CRAWLING

Looking at billions of products and websites is hard work, and there definitely isn't a chap sat in a chair 24 hours a day, manually reading them all. So they send in little bots to do it for them. These bots read the information you submitted through your SEO efforts, and then index accordingly. This means next time someone searches for something, these little bots have already previously done the hard work and produce the results they need. Gold star to these little bots.

If you are not using SEO correctly, or at all, then you may find that your website or shop is deathly quiet, with little or no views and sales. On-site SEO (more on this shortly) would be one of the first places I would suggest to look if you are wanting to drive more traffic to your website.

So before we dive into the nitty gritty of SEO, let's look at the shopper journey a little bit closer, to learn more on how this works in real time:

1. Shopper lands on a search engine

2. They search for what they think they want

3. They are shown a set of results that isn't really want they want

4. They narrow their search by adding more words

5. They see a different set of results

6. They may narrow it down again or change their search

7. They finally find what they are looking for

8. They click on a website/product

9. They review and shortlist the product

10. They buy or leave.

That is a basic overview of how a shopper would search; now let's look at a real-life example of this (get a video representation in the Book Bonuses that you can download at www.handmadebosses.com/bookbonus).

1. Alice is looking for a t-shirt for her best friend who is a new mum so she searches "t-shirt" on Etsy.

2. She is greeted with 389,976 results, and sees all sorts of styles and types of t-shirt in her search - not what she is after.

3. She adds "new mum" into the search box to make the search "new mum t-shirt" and hits enter.

4. Better, but still not what she is after.

5. She thinks hard and realises that her friend only wears white t-shirts. She edits her search to "white t-shirt for new mum".

6. She starts to see some great t-shirts, especially one that has a funny slogan. It's right up her friend's street, but wants to see more.

7. She changes her search finally to "funny t-shirt for new mum in white".

8. Ah-ha! She finds a great one, orders and pays.

This is a basic version of how searching works on a platform like Etsy, Amazon and Ebay. These are similar, but SEO on your own website can be a bit harder, although not impossible. This is because there are thousands more results on Google, than on a marketplace like Etsy, so you are in essence competing with more people. This is where off-site and on-site SEO come in:

- on-site SEO - things you can do to your own website and products to make them more discoverable. Optimising "image alt text" (a text description of your images that search engines look at to determine what it is - search engines don't have eyeballs!), titles, internal links and descriptions all count as on-site SEO.
- off-site SEO - things you can do to bring traffic to your website and increase its authority in search engines such as social posts and external links. Search engines look for outside higher-ranking websites to link to your website to show that your website is trustworthy. So, for example, if an allrecipes.com article was to link to chopping boards on your website, this would show search engines that your site is obviously pretty good, and will show it higher in search results over other websites.

Luckily, most handmade business owners will naturally build up their off-site SEO with marketing anyway, but on-site SEO can be a bit more hands-on. You should be focusing your efforts on:

- titles - make sure that you have search terms in your title that your target market would use, but make sure it still makes sense
- tags - (if a marketplace uses them) these are often used as a further tool to enable the marketplace search to rank and list your items; use keyword terms that your target market would commonly use
- descriptions - (the beginning matters most) sprinkle your keywords in the description, in a way that makes sense

- image alt text - describe the image using keywords
- internal links - link to other products or content within your website or store
- up to date and relevant content and info - keeping your website up to date is vital
- load speed - make sure your website doesn't take too long to load. If it does, try deleting apps, rogue code or high-res videos or images. Remember, simple is always better!

Ok Boss, so you know now where you should be focusing your efforts and why, but HOW do we actually do this? How do we find those all-important keywords? Well first thing to note here is that there are millions of word combos and ways people use to describe your items out there, so a large portion of this is going to be trial and error and testing (sorry!) but here's a Boss's step-by-step guide to finding keywords that will get you views:

Coaching Questions:

STEP 1 Why do people buy your item?

Make a list of occasions and reasons why people buy your item.

Who for?

What would they use it for?

How do people in your niche describe what you have to sell?

Are there any "out of the box" ways to describe it?

STEP 2 How would people describe your item?

What words would they use?

What phrases would they use?

What kind of mindset would they be in when looking for your item?

STEP 3 Can you add qualifying keywords to these phrases to make them more specific and long-tail? For example "wool" and "hat" may become "black wool hat with rim" or "black wool Trilby hat".

STEP 7 Look at the place you intend to sell on (or marketplace); what kind of keywords are being used in other listings?

What is your competition doing?

How are they describing what you sell?

How are they describing their products on their social media channels?

STEP 5 check other product search engines like Pinterest, Etsy, Amazon and see what comes up there for your item.

STEP 6 out of these lists of phrases, what's relevant to your business?

Which ones wouldn't make sense for you to use?

What products would the user intend to find with this search?

If there are common themes, group 5-13 of them together in a "keyword group"

CHAPTER 12 : KICK-BUTT KEYWORDS

STEP 7 Which of these phrases has a high number of searches each month and a low amount of searches?

Rank these phrases using tools like Keywords Everywhere and Google Keyword Planner. If you are selling on Etsy, you can use the free or paid version of eRank to do all this for you.

Hint: you ideally want to test a mixture of low, medium and high searched phrases. (Download the full maker toolkit with loads of SEO tools at www.handmadebosses.com/bookbonus)

STEP 8 Which of these phrases have a low competition (a fewer number of websites are using them)?

Rank these phrases using tools like Keywords Everywhere, Google Results and Google Keyword Planner. If you are selling on Etsy, you can use the free or paid version of eRank to do this all for you.

Hint: you ideally want to test a mixture of low, medium and highly competitive phrases.

STEP 9 If you grouped your keywords together, consider creating separate listings (on marketplaces) or different listings (on your own website) for different keyword focuses. For example, having a listing with a focus of "gift for friend" and another for "personalised wooden plaque".

STEP 10 Change your SEO or list the new items and leave them for three months. Make a note of the review dates and change nothing until you have given it a chance to be crawled and indexed by the platform you're using. SEO is a long-term game, not a short-term gain, after all.

STEP 11 after 3-4 months, come back and review what keywords have done well for you.

Make a note of them and create other listings (or edit the existing one) and re-use the "good" keywords, and replace the "bad" keywords by going through the process again, or using your list from step six.

(NOTE: If you are selling on Etsy, don't change your SEO until your listing expires, and don't change SEO on a listing that's working for you. Always COPY the listings and do this).

Ok, so now we have a good idea of a strategy to find great keywords, but let's recap with some quick do's and don'ts:

SEO DO'S AND DON'TS

Don'ts:

- don't change your SEO every week, leave it for at least three months to get an accurate representation of how it's doing
- don't keyword-stuff or use unnatural language
- don't put all of your SEO efforts into one page and shove all of your keywords on one page, "sprinkle" them naturally throughout your site/shop
- don't pay someone from Upwork or Fiverr for backlinks or cheap optimisation - slow and steady wins the race; there are no shortcuts here
- don't set it and forget it; SEO is changing constantly so make sure to stay up to date

Do's:

- do optimise image alt text if you can
- do use quality links to link to other pages within your site
- do have different keyword focuses and groups
- do track performance
- do use long-tail keywords

- do use relevant and related searches
- do consider what the user intent is
- do make sure your website has a speedy loading time (under three seconds is optimal)

SEO is not the be-all-and-end-all of having a successful handmade online business. It's just ONE of the 50-plus cog machine that needs to be well-oiled enough to run as a successful business. Don't let anyone tell you that SEO is the only thing you need to be focusing on - this is a huge mistake and probably one of the worst I have seen. Remember, you could have the best SEO in the world and still not convert viewers into buyers.

Student Stories

"Here is how HBSA helped me with SEO.

"I opened my Etsy shop in June 2020 and looking back now, I knew so little about what SEO was and how it worked on Etsy and beyond. When listing each kit, I would simply describe what each kit was, for instance a "sewing kit" or a "craft kit".

"Joining HBSA has really opened my eyes as to how SEO works and how Etsy uses it to rank listings. HBSA reinforces how important it is to know who your target market is and how they might search for the things you sell, teaching us that there is no "one size fits all" when it comes to keywords. HBSA has also suggested and helped me find so many other categories and ways to list products, for instance occasion gifting, celebrations and gifts for different groups of individuals. By creating listings and using researched

SEO for lots of different categories all within my target market, my Etsy shop has grown enormously.

"SEO research is (secretly) quite an enjoyable part of owning my Etsy shop, it allows me to really dig deep into the mindsets of my customers and research how they find me and therefore how future potential customers can too. Once you understand how it works, and what steps to take, SEO research can be fun and extremely financially rewarding for your Etsy shop, and HBSA has taken me by the hand and really helped me develop mine."

- Tamsin Parker, The Orchid Craft Room.

WHAT ARE YOUR thoughts?

Chapter 13

MAGICAL YET MANAGEABLE MARKETING

Marketing, advertising or promoting your products can seem like a whole different ball game in itself, and you're not wrong, Boss. When our thousands of bosses were surveyed, marketing was in the top three things that they still felt they needed to master. In this chapter, we're going to create a marketing plan of sorts for your business, but first, let's look at what marketing is in a bit more detail.

A bit like SEO, marketing can strike fear into the hearts of budding handmade bosses everywhere, but really it's just connecting the right people with the right product at the right time in a way that you can control. It's really not any more complicated than that.

All business owners have to be marketers by default, and if the word "marketing" really leaves you feeling like you have to take a hot shower, think of it this way: you have been marketing since you were born. When you pleaded with your parents for that birthday gift and gave a plethora of reasons as to why you need it - that's marketing. When you tried to convince that friend to come with you for a late-night trip to McDonalds drive through - marketing.

What about the interview for that job you really wanted? Oh yes, marketing. Whether you like the word or not (change

Space for your notes

it to another word like "flooping the wompers" if you want to #soprofessional) you have actually been marketing your whole life. People often get bogged down by marketing and promotion because they think it's for sleazeballs in £1000 suits, but really it's just about putting your best foot forward to people who have a desire for what you have.

100 TRUE FANS VS 5000 GHOSTERS

Something that deserves a little space of its own is this (and as I have mentioned before because it's just SO important): it's better to have 100 true fans rather than 5000 people that don't really care about you or your business or that don't connect with you in any way. Resist the temptation to grow vanity metrics quickly, but grow them slow and steady instead. So many people focus on follower numbers, subscribers and viewers but don't actually take the time to look at the quality of the traffic coming in. You will get a better conversion rate. It's far better to get 10 true fans a month, than 1000 people who aren't bothered.

Note: Just as a reminder, your conversion rate is how many people buy/convert/sign up/do an action you want them to out of how many people view, expressed as a percentage. If 100 people view and one person buys, that's 1%. If 250 people view and three buy, that's 1.2%. Conversion rate can be worked out by dividing the purchases/sign-ups by the viewers, and multiply by 100

Views / Conversions x 100

Many failed business owners will state that a lack of marketing was the downfall of their business, but really, it's usually something much simpler than that. Having worked with many, many handmade business owners, the most common five reasons for failure are actually:

- lack of passion for your business
- not understanding target market
- not relating the product to the target market well enough
- not telling enough people about your product
- profitability issues

All of these we will have addressed in this book, so you Boss, are already miles ahead of everyone who hasn't read this book - Yay!

When you are starting a marketing effort, there are two main steps to it:

1. Write a marketing plan

2. Decide where you want to market

Rinse and repeat, it's as simple as that.

DOING IT ALL

"You cannot do it all!" should be something that all business owners take the time to really embed in their minds. Although it can be tempting to try and do all the things and say yes to everything, really the key is learning what's worth your efforts. Something I would recommend is treating each marketing avenue (a place where you market) as its own separate branch of the business. If a branch is performing poorly, you cut it off and use the time/energy/finances for something else. This is why you should focus on ONE marketing avenue at a time.

Yep, ONE. It can be so alluring to do 2, 3, 4, 5 or even 6 at a time to try and make more money, but it will actually have the opposite effect. By mastering one avenue first, you are actually making sure that you first build a long-term source of traffic before you move on; by doing this, you reduce the risk of failure and revenue dips. This goes for social media too: only start ONE social media platform at a time, spend 4-6 months on it, master it, understand it fully, and make sure you're getting a great ROI (Return On Investment) before you move on.

Some clues that indicate whether you've mastered one marketing stream:

- you get consistent targeted traffic to your store
- you get sales from that platform or marketing channel
- your efforts get lots of engagement and clicks
- you get comments asking for more like this, or praise
- you find it naturally easy to get views from it
- your target market are on the platform in their droves

OK, so let's get building your marketing plan. You should revisit and revise this every time you have a big marketing push. I would advise that you have a big marketing push before you need revenue coming in, for example before a quiet time like January-March, (I call this "slump marketing"), or before a big sales period to give momentum and boost your sales like October-December, (I call this "momentum marketing"). It really depends on your marketing goals.

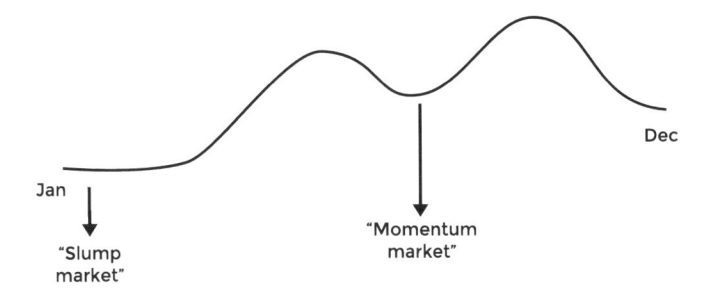

Jan — "Slump market"

"Momentum market"

Dec

Coaching Questions:

Build a marketing plan

1. **Revisit and understand your target audience.** Use your ideal target customer from before to remind yourself who your product is for, what their pain point is, why they need your product, and how it relates to them.

2. **Get into the hideouts.** Now we have revisited your target market, let's look at where they hang out based on the target market assumptions we made. Where does your target market consume information?

What information do they consume?

What communities do they belong to?

Where do they hang out online?

How could you reach them?

3. **Truly understand your offer.** What you make gives something to a customer, it solves a pain point for them in some way, so let's dig a little deeper. What does your product actually do?

How does it deliver?

What pain points does it address?

What is its USP? What is your brand USP?

What do you understand about your target market that no-one else does?

4. **Break down the plan.** What do you want/need from this marketing effort?

How many sales?

How much revenue?

How many products would you have to sell to meet this?

Will new or existing customers be interested in this?

How would you market to both existing customers and/or new customers?

What will be the biggest customer objections they would have?

How long will you run/measure this for?

5. **Tell the world.** This is the step where so many business owners procrastinate. When you know where to go to find your target market, what message to bring to the table and how to deliver it, this is the time to actually get on and do it.

When will you start promoting?

How will you do it?

Will you use testimonials?

Will you use images or video?

How long will you run the promotion or marketing avenue before measuring?

When do you want to start seeing results?

6. **Measure.** After you have pressed the big red button on your marketing efforts, make a plan to measure it daily.

How many views has it had?

How many people engaged?

How many people clicked?

How many people bought?

7. **Analyse.** Look at the data you collected in the last step, does it meet expectations?

Exceed them?

What's working?

What's not?

Are there any common issues or questions?

8. **Pivot.** You can pivot whilst the promotion or marketing effort is happening - what needs to be changed quickly?

What can you tweak to make this perform better?

9. **Cut the dead branches.** After the time frame expires that you set out in Step 4, look at how it has gone so far/how it went. Would you do it again?

Did it meet your goals?

Was it easy to do?

Is it something you will do on a permanent basis?

What did it bring to you?

Did it help brand awareness?

If you find something that didn't perform well enough, or wasn't worth the effort, don't think twice about cutting it.

10.   Rinse and repeat. When will you repeat this process?

So, now let's look at some great beginner places to market your pieces:

- social media - Facebook, Pinterest, TikTok, Twitter, Instagram, Clubhouse etc
- influencers - bloggers, You Tubers, Instagrammers
- guest post - on blogs, forums, Facebook groups etc
- social media interaction - through social media posts and questions
- email marketing - sell through an email
- existing customers in your social media channels
- content marketing - blog posts, videos, carousel posts, reels, stories
- affiliates - paying someone a % of sales they drive to you

Let's go deeper into some of those bullet points for some of my favourite marketing techniques:

SOCIAL MEDIA

Let me say this once - you do not have to add a gruelling social media posting schedule to your task list. Many business owners shy away from social media because they think they have to be posting 2-3 times a day. I'm happy to report that through years of testing, it's about quality rather than quantity. Some of the most successful brands on the planet post twice a week, but they make sure that those posts pack a punch with their target market.

Again, like other marketing methods, I would recommend choosing and mastering ONE social media network at a time to work on. Many of my students find true success with one, and have that as their main source of leads.

INFLUENCERS

Through leveraging other people's networks and followers you can gain access to ready-primed people waiting for a product like yours. Some influencers will require a fee, whilst some will publish a blog post, video or social post in exchange for the item only. Do your due diligence and be sure to research previous posts, engagement, and other brands they have worked with in the past before you invest. If you're unsure whether to send an item to an influencer or not, a good rule of thumb is to assume 5-10% of people who engage with a post will click, and 1-2% of those people will buy from you.

♡👍 1000 → 10% → 🖱 100 → 1-2% → £$ 1-2 Sales

Make sure to manage expectations with influencer communities - remember, they are used to being sold to, so may come to expect or ignore those kinds of posts.

GUEST POSTING

As we have discovered, education through content and positioning yourself as an authoritative source within your niche are two must-do's to ensure your businesses longevity. This is just a fancy way of saying "teach to build trust". The best way to do that to the masses (and get access to a load of eyeballs at the same time) is to guest-post. This is great for related blogs and information sources for your target audience. Not only does it expose you to your target market, but it also shows how knowledgeable you are in the niche you sell. Approach common blogs and places where your target market goes for information, think outside the box at how linked subject matters can attract people who would love your product. For example, someone who sells soy wax candles could create a blog post for a home-owner magazine, talking about what your house smell says about you,.

SOCIAL MEDIA INTERACTION

Have you ever gone onto social media with the aim of just being...social? Many people go to Facebook groups, Instagram accounts and Pinterest boards with the aim of getting answers and to be inspired. Why not be their source of contact? Answering questions within Facebook groups, commenting on the posts of your competitors' followers, and direct-messaging someone with a helpful response to their post are all great ways to become a great source of information, and the go-to person people will think of when they need something

AFFILIATES

Affiliate marketing is essentially where you get someone else to market for you, in exchange for a cut of the revenue received. You can do this through your own website using an add-on or a cart software like Kartra, or you can manually track names and email addresses through orders. You can even get affiliates to host in-person evenings and meet-ups to sell your products physically.

MAIL MARKETING

Email marketing is a whole different board game, albeit something I recommend every business owner do. Building a list of interested people means you essentially own your very own list of people wanting to hear from you and buy from you. Sending focused and specific marketing emails to these people is a great way to receive revenue on demand, and to promote coupons, collection launches and new products.

CONTENT MARKETING

Probably pretty self-explanatory, but creating helpful content around what your target market is searching for is a great way to encourage people into your business. For example, an organic t-shirt maker could create a blog post on why organic cotton is better for your skin. Another great benefit to this is that it drives traffic to your website, and if you include comments or links to related products, to them too.

So now we have an idea of where we want to market and a plan for it, it's time for you to go ahead and start digging into some marketing tests. Many coaches will encourage you to do specific types of marketing and ignore the rest, however in my experience what works for one business won't work for another. Armed with your marketing plan, test and track your marketing efforts and learn what works well for your business.

Coaching Questions:

Where will you focus your marketing efforts?

What will you do?

How do you need to prepare?

Who do you need to contact?

Any other notes?

To recap, let's go over some do's and don'ts of marketing.

DO'S:
- treat each platform, marketing idea and promotion method as its own business branch
- be strict with cutting off branches that are not getting you a decent ROI (anything over 2.5x)
- consider whether the audience of a particular platform or person will actually be interested in your product
- make sure to research a platform's target market first
- have a strong message for your marketing channel that links in with your target market's pain point/worry
- be yourself. Don't put on another persona, always be yourself
- share reviews and praise from others for your business
- encourage interaction by asking questions
- make sure that your profile and linked social media channels are updated and relevant
- ensure that your logo and branding are updated and consistent across all marketing efforts
- use video and "lives" wherever possible - these often get pushed to the top of feeds

DON'TS

- don't start a marketing campaign just because someone else has
- don't copy a competitor's marketing campaign - you don't know what goes on behind the scenes
- don't set vague goals for a marketing effort
- don't ignore your own business hashtags, make sure to search them regularly to catch what other people are saying about your business
- don't create each post as and when, batch them for optimum time hacking
- don't ignore comments and messages from customers
- don't always sell to your customers, intersperse it with other types of content too
- don't post strong views on current issues, news or politics. You may lose followers from people who are just there to shop
- don't post derogatory things about your competition.

Chapter 14

SIMPLY SCALING + TAKE YOUR BUSINESS FURTHER

Wowzers! We have gone on one heck of a journey throughout this book. By now you should have notes scribbled throughout, a good sense of what you need to do to start making regular sales, and an appetite and love for your business like never before. But what now? Where do we go from here?

Firstly, if you haven't already, don't forget to download the Book Bonuses for some hands-on tools, resources and extra bits that will help you in your journey. You can download that at www.handmadebosses.com/bookbonus

Well, the simple answer is: scale. Scaling is essentially where we have a business, or an element in our business that works, and we just scale it up. It's a bit like making a cake that's double the size, you just double the recipe. That's exactly what it means to scale a business, you're just ramping up efforts that work already. Do you notice that people loved your in-progress video? Do more of it and share it far and wide. Do you notice that people love it when you build hype and launch product collections at the same time? Do more of it!

Space for your notes

Coaching Questions:

What has worked well for you over the last month?

What has worked well for you over the last 3 months?

What has brought you targeted traffic over the last 12 months?

How can you incorporate more of that in the next 12 months of your business?

Basically, do more of what already works. That being said, there is always more you could be doing for sure.

Creating a handmade business that is successful is a bit like a puzzle. You won't have all of the pieces in your grasp when you begin, a year in or even two years in. There will always be something just out of reach, something missing which could catapult your business further.

This could be a marketing effort, an understanding of something, a strategy for one particular aspect of your business, or simply a coach to help you through it all. That is where Handmade Bosses comes in. Myself and my team are dedicated to helping handmade businesses take over online retail, and have a plethora of resources and knowledge at our disposal. We would love to have you join our various coaching opportunities and courses too, all of which can be found at www.handmadebosses.com.

I'm so proud of you Boss, now you are officially a handmade boss and a world of satisfying creative work awaits you.

WHAT ARE YOUR *thoughts?*

Printed in Great Britain
by Amazon